TAKE CARE OF YOUR DOG
WITH THE
HOME VET HANDBOOK

TAKE CARE OF YOUR
DOG

HOME VET HANDBOOKS

Text by Margaret Crush.
Illustrations by John Gosler.
Veterinary consultant Michael Findlay
BVMS, MRCVS.

Printed in the United States of America.
Library of Congress Cataloguing in
Publication Data: 83-619-64

Contents

5

Record chart

Record sheet for your dog

Name

Date of birth
(actual or estimated)

Breed   Sex

Colour/description

Photograph

Notes on feeding   Medical notes   Breeding record or
                                                date of neutering operation

Veterinary surgeon   Surgery hours

Practice address   Tel No

Vaccination record

	Date	Age of puppy	Veterinary surgeon
Distemper			
Leptospirosis			
Canine Parvovirus			
Canine Hepatitis			

Booster injections: dates

This book has been prepared under expert veterinary guidance to help you — the concerned layman who wants to do the best for his dog. In many cases you will know that there is something wrong with your dog but not be sure whether it is serious enough to warrant a visit to the vet — on the other hand you don't want to neglect something which may be serious. To help you in just this situation you'll find the following pages include a flow chart for each major part of your dog's body. The top row of boxes contains a variety of different symptoms that you are likely to notice first. Having chosen the most appropriate of these, move down to the middle boxes which contain a number of alternative accompanying symptoms. Once you've picked the one most relevant to the animal's complaint, you should be able to tell what might be wrong with your dog. The panels containing the answers will be one of three different shapes — see our example below for what they mean.

Always check your dog over very carefully for any other signs of illness which may not be immediately apparent, because many complaints appear very similar to unprofessional eyes unless *all* the symptoms are taken into account. Also remember that even if the initial suggestion is that you try treating the dog at home, you must always consult the vet if the problem persists for more than a few days or if the dog's condition gets worse. Naturally, you don't want to tamper with his health unnecessarily, so always go to the vet if you're in any doubt or can't diagnose the cause of the problem. Your vet would much rather you contacted him than risk unnecessary suffering. However, there will be occasions when you can save the vet's time, and yourself bills, by treating minor ailments at home.

Moreover, it will often be your responsibility to carry out the vet's advice and treatment at home and pages 34-37 give helpful advice on nursing your dog back to health. Sometimes your — or someone else's — dog may be involved in an accident, so on pages 38-45 you'll find simple, practical advice on first-aid treatment which may be vital in saving the life of a much-loved pet.

Finally, the last section of the book tells you how to look after your dog from day to day, because a healthy dog is, more often than not, a cared-for dog. Food, housing, training and other helpful hints on good dog management are included, as well as advice on coping with a pregnant female and her puppies.

So, with some helpful advice and a little luck, here's to a happy and, above all, healthy dog.

If answer is in a rectangular panel, the complaint is something you can treat yourself — for a while at least

If answer is in a many-sided panel, you can do something to alleviate the problems while getting an appointment with the vet

If answer is in a circular panel, you should go to the vet immediately

Getting a vet

The following are times when you and your dog *really* need a vet, but if you are not sure whether his problem comes into one of these categories, see the vet anyway — just to be on the safe side. If you live a long way from any vet, remember there's always the telephone, so keep his number on hand just as you keep your doctor's for yourself and your family.

- Any emergency — see pages 38-45
- When you have tried to treat the dog at home for a short while as suggested and he isn't improving — or is getting worse.
- When any condition (even an apparently non-serious one) has gone on too long.
- Any problem that appears to need X-ray, laboratory analysis of droppings, urine or vomit, or anaesthetics.
- Any problem needing drugs (including antibiotics).
- Difficult pregnancy or labor.
- Castration or spaying (neutering).
- Vaccinations.
- Check-ups.
- Euthanasia.

Finally, don't expect the vet to always be a miracle-worker. Often he or she does save the seemingly hopeless case but, like doctors, vets sometimes have patients who, despite all treatment, cannot be saved — and then they feel just as depressed as you do.

Home treatment

Treating your dog at home is possible, and necessary, for a range of minor ailments and injuries. Simple first aid is also something which the owner should be able to carry out. However, you should remember that animals have no way of describing to you how they feel, and you have no foolproof method of deciding what is wrong with them. This book will help you to assess your dog's health, but it is not intended to be a substitute for professional veterinary advice.

Vets the world over are highly qualified medical practitioners, invariably sympathetic to owner's problems and always concerned about your animal's welfare. They will give you the best possible advice and instruction on the care of your dog, and home treatment is always best carried out under veterinary advice — except for very minor ailments.

Choosing a vet

As soon as you acquire a dog or pup, get yourself a vet — don't wait until you have an emergency to deal with, because then you won't necessarily make the wisest choice.

Apart from the likelihood that you'll need him at some future date, you should get the vet to check over a new dog or puppy immediately and give him the appropriate inoculations. This will give you a chance to see if you like the vet and his methods, his office and assistants. Make sure you feel confident with him and are in sympathy with his attitude to your dog. Vets vary in just the same way as doctors — and you and your dog will get on much better with a vet you trust and like, so it's worth taking the trouble to find one you feel comfortable with. No matter how medically qualified or experienced he or she is, you need to be at ease with your vet and to feel that the two of you are working well together in the best interest of that all-important third party — your dog.

Questions you might ask yourself are:
Does the vet appear uninterested in your pet? If so, look elsewhere.
Does the vet explain things in terms that you can understand? If he doesn't or assumes knowledge you don't possess, ask for clarification then and there. It's much better than having to call up after hours or, worse, to do the wrong thing to the unfortunate dog.
Do the vet and his assistants seem calm and efficient when handling nervous animals?
When you call, does the receptionist ask you for brief details of the problem to help decide whether you must bring the dog in then and there, or if it can 'wait until morning'?
Do the other people and animals in the waiting room seem happy about going to see the vet?
Are good records kept about your dog?
Does the vet provide an emergency service himself or an answering service to find out where you can get this?
What facilities are offered — X-ray unit, operating room, etc?
Lastly, are the clinic and waiting room spotless?

When you have found your vet, remember to be courteous and punctual in your appointments and come prepared with as many facts about the dog's illness and relevant samples as you can. The vet will want to know when the condition first appeared, what the signs were, whether the dog has had a high temperature and so on. And if you can provide relevant samples of urine, stool or vomit, this will be invaluable to him. Also remember to keep a sick dog warm and dry on his way to the vet or his condition may worsen.

Don't disturb the vet at night unless *absolutely* essential, and don't expect a diagnosis over the phone (you must keep your part of the bargain and take the trouble to bring the dog into the pet hospital if the vet asks you to). Never, because of a possible high bill, delay taking an animal to the vet for several days, as it could cost more in the long run, and your vet will also find it very frustrating if an animal dies simply because it hasn't received treatment soon enough.

The healthy dog

When you buy a new dog, this diagram should help you check over his "vital statistics." It will also help you to keep an eye on your existing dog's health — if you are in doubt about this, turn to page 12 and work through the check list.

COAT

Clean and well groomed. Free from parasites, eggs or droppings, loose hairs or scurf. No bald patches in coat. No spots, sores or scale on coat or hair-free belly.

ANUS

Like hair of hind legs, should be clean and not fouled with loose droppings. No sign of diarrhea.

ABDOMEN

Not distended (no pot belly). No wounds, growths or sores.

FEET

Should have no tears, thorns, splinters or damaged pads. Claws not broken.

Vaccination

This is essential to protect your dog against killer diseases like distemper. You should get a vaccination certificate with the dog. If not — or if you're in any doubt — have him vaccinated again, and keep up the booster shots — see page 61.

EARS

Clean with no discharge. Breeds with naturally upright ears should have them pricked and alert.

Other Points to Watch

Appetite should be good. Find out what diet the dog has been on.
Breathing should be quiet and normal. No coughing or sneezing.
Droppings — neither sloppy nor hard. Not pale.
Behavior should be lively, alert and friendly. Don't choose the shy, nervous pup at the back of the kennel.
Movements — lively, no limping, etc.
Take the dog to your vet for a general check-up as soon as you get him home.

EYES

Clear and not bloodshot. No discharge. Inside eyelids should be pink. Third eyelid not unduly visible.

NOSE

Clean with no discharge, although a clear drop of water is acceptable. Nose should be cool.

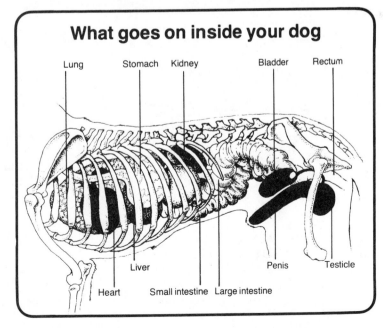

What goes on inside your dog

Lung   Stomach   Kidney   Bladder   Rectum

Liver   Penis   Testicle

Heart   Small intestine   Large intestine

The sick dog

The opposite page shows where you can expect to find the appropriate advice for a range of common diseases and ailments. Further information can be found in the sections headed *First Aid for Your dog, The Happy Event,* etc. Remember not to rush into a diagnosis — the charts which follow are intended to be a general guide to the health of your dog, not an instant diagnostic process. If you have the slightest suspicion that your dog may be suffering from one of the more serious ailments, a visit to the vet will probably set your mind at rest — either because the trouble is not as bad as you feared, or because the vet is able to administer the correct treatment.

The most common signs of illness are a change of behavior or appetite, high temperature, dehydration and a weak pulse. Similarly, if you notice your dog has become quieter than usual or is shivering when not frightened or cold,

these could also be taken as signs that all may not well.

Apart from keeping a watchful eye over your dog for signs of illness, there's a lot you can do to prevent him from becoming sick in the first place. For a start you can make sure that he's inoculated against distemper, canine hepatitis, etc., and also remember to keep up the booster shots to ensure his resistance to these viruses. Checking his coat every day for ticks and other external parasites will also prevent a serious infestation or infection, and keeping him on a regular, nourishing diet will do further wonders for his health and appearance. However, even with all your loving care, there may still be occasions when your dog seems ill and you're not sure whether or not to take him to the vet. Work through this list of general symptoms, and turn to the relevant pages for further information to help you pinpoint this trouble.

Don't take risks with your dog's health – if you're in any doubt at all about his problem go to the vet. It's better to be safe than sorry.

SOURCE OF TROUBLE	SYMPTOMS	PAGE
The ears	Dog scratching, shaking head, discharge from ears, evidence of swelling.	PAGE 14
The eyes	Inflammation, discharge, dog pawing at eye/s, film over eye, swelling.	PAGE 16
The fur and skin	Unusual fur or skin condition, scratching, swelling, patches in fur.	PAGE 18
Genitals	Discharge, frequent urination, excessive thirst, vomiting and/or diarrhea.	PAGE 20
Limbs, Muscles	Lameness or unusual movement, swollen joints, partial/total paralysis.	PAGE 22
Mouth and teeth	Excessive salivation, dog pawing at mouth, inflammation or swelling, loss of appetite.	PAGE 24
The nose	Sneezing, discharge from nose and/or eyes, high temperature.	PAGE 26
The respiratory system	Labored/wheezy breathing, discharge from eyes/nose, inflammation of throat, high temperature, lethargy.	PAGE 28
The stomach	Vomiting and/or diarrhea, constipation, abnormal thirst, blood in stools or vomit, high temperature.	PAGE 30
Waterworks	Excessive or less frequent urination, blood in urine, severe thirst, smelly breath, dog straining and in pain after urinating.	PAGE 32

The ears

Clean ears are much less prone to developing ear trouble, so if necessary, clean your dog's ears once a week with a cotton swab, such as a Q-tip (see panel). However, most ear complaints should have the vet's attention in the early stages, because they can be difficult to eradicate once established. Effective emergency treatment is to pour large amounts of liquid paraffin, warmed to blood heat, down the ear canal, which will soothe acute inflammation.

Special collars

To prevent a dog from aggravating any ear infection, you can fit him out with a special collar (see illustration) made from thin cardboard. This will prevent him from scratching the affected area, but most dogs won't take kindly to such an appliance, so only use one if really necessary.

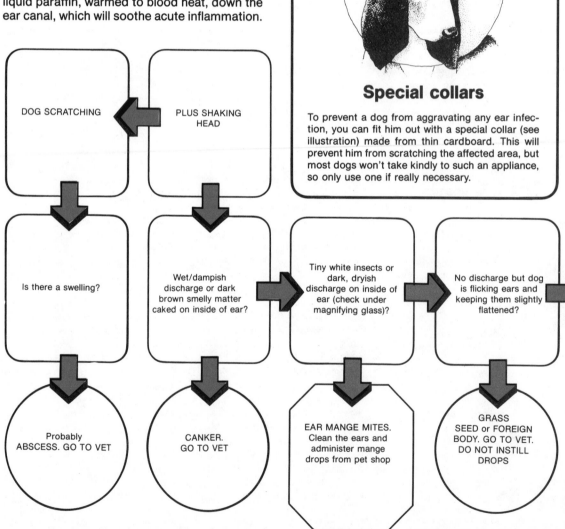

DOG SCRATCHING ← PLUS SHAKING HEAD

Is there a swelling?

→ Probably ABSCESS. GO TO VET

Wet/dampish discharge or dark brown smelly matter caked on inside of ear? →

CANKER. GO TO VET

Tiny white insects or dark, dryish discharge on inside of ear (check under magnifying glass)? →

EAR MANGE MITES. Clean the ears and administer mange drops from pet shop

No discharge but dog is flicking ears and keeping them slightly flattened? →

GRASS SEED or FOREIGN BODY. GO TO VET. DO NOT INSTILL DROPS

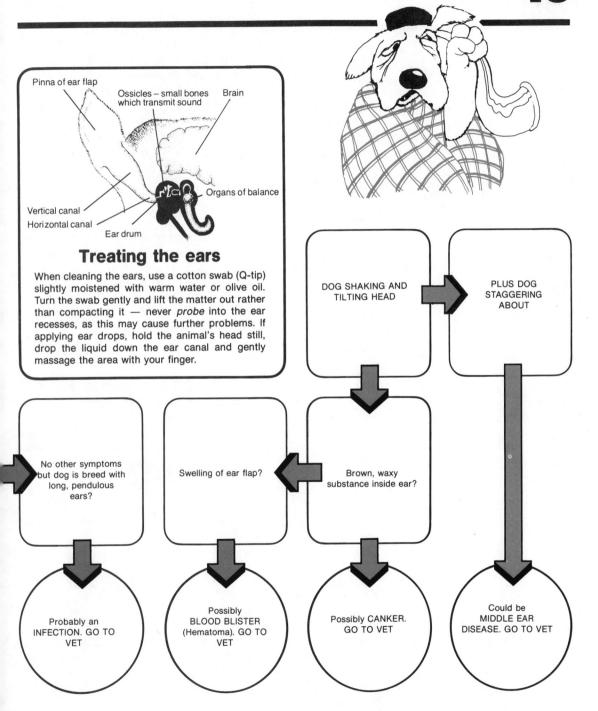

Treating the ears

When cleaning the ears, use a cotton swab (Q-tip) slightly moistened with warm water or olive oil. Turn the swab gently and lift the matter out rather than compacting it — never *probe* into the ear recesses, as this may cause further problems. If applying ear drops, hold the animal's head still, drop the liquid down the ear canal and gently massage the area with your finger.

Pinna of ear flap

Ossicles – small bones which transmit sound

Brain

Organs of balance

Vertical canal

Horizontal canal

Ear drum

DOG SHAKING AND TILTING HEAD

PLUS DOG STAGGERING ABOUT

No other symptoms but dog is breed with long, pendulous ears?

Swelling of ear flap?

Brown, waxy substance inside ear?

Probably an INFECTION. GO TO VET

Possibly BLOOD BLISTER (Hematoma). GO TO VET

Possibly CANKER. GO TO VET

Could be MIDDLE EAR DISEASE. GO TO VET

The eyes

The eye is a very delicate organ and shouldn't be messed around with if you are not sure what you are doing. If in any doubt, go to the vet, as mild conditions can deteriorate quite quickly. Do not put anything in or near the eye that is not specifically labeled for ophthalmic use (particularly antiseptics), and don't use an old eye preparation left over from a previous occasion. Growths or swellings in the area of the eyes need immediate veterinary attention, as they may spread or cause other complications.

TEAR STAINS BELOW EYES

EYES SORE, RUNNY, MATTERY OR WEEPING

Removing a foreign body

Try to remove the object with tweezers or a cotton swab (Q-tip) if visible. If not, bathe the eyes every few hours and administer eye ointment. If the complaint persists, go to the vet. Laceration of the eyeball itself or penetration by a foreign body is very serious and should receive the vet's attention immediately. Don't try to remove anything imbedded in the eye yourself — leave it to the vet.

Symptoms in one eye only; dog pawing at eye?

OR

Inflamed eyelids?

OR

Discharge from both eyes and nose, high temperature?

Could be BLOCKED TEAR DUCTS or INFOLDED EYELID. GO TO VET

Probably FOREIGN BODY. See panel

Probably CONJUNCTIVITIS. GO TO VET

Could be serious. GO TO VET IMMEDIATELY

How to apply eyedrops

Tilt dog's head back and pull lower eyelid down slightly. Drop the lotion from its own applicator into the inner corner of eye. Continue to hold the head back for a moment or two while the drops disperse over the whole eye surface. Do not touch the eye itself with the dropper.

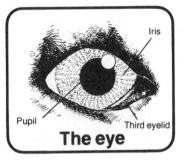

The eye

Iris

Pupil

Third eyelid

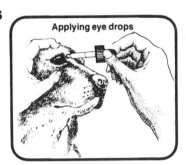

Applying eye drops

REMEMBER

Any symptom lasting more than one day warrants a visit to the vet – don't take risks with your dog's eyes. The safest eye wash is boiled water raised to blood heat; the most useful first aid dressing is castor oil.

SUDDEN PAIN

BLUE/WHITE FILM OVER ONE OR BOTH EYES

OR

Enlargement of third eyelid (see diagram)?

Injury to eyeball from thorns, fighting, etc.?

OR

Increase in size of eyeball?

PROLAPSED THIRD EYELID. Should clear up in a few days, if not GO TO VET

Moisten eye with castor oil. Place cotton pad soaked in castor oil over eye, then dry surrounding hair and eyelids and GO TO VET. (See panel)

Possibly GLAUCOMA. GO TO VET

Probably INFLAMMATION OF THE CORNEA. GO TO VET

The fur and skin

A great majority of the problems with your dog's fur and skin will come as the result of some parasitic infestation, but don't jump to conclusions and start covering him in flea powder and the like. Dietary deficiencies can also produce a poor coat, so keep your dog on a regular and well-balanced diet, which will do a lot to improve his health and appearance. As always, prevention is better than cure, and daily grooming will help keep his skin problems to a minimum.

External parasites

Apart from fleas, there are a number of other parasites that will live on dogs if given the chance, the most serious of which is the tick (see page 42). These must be eradicated as soon as possible, as should any similar creatures that may take a liking to your dog, including lice, various species of mites, chiggers and stickfast fleas.

PLUS SCRATCHING ← BALD PATCHES IN FUR

Patches on forehead, neck or forelegs; skin thickened, grey, wrinkled and possibly smelly? **OR**

Patches on lower back and base of tail; skin dry, reddish and covered in tiny black scabs? **OR**

Patches on edge of ears and elsewhere; skin thick, crusty, grey and scaley?

Patches not completely bare; skin dry, white and flaky; dog otherwise normal?

DEMODECTIC MANGE. GO TO VET

FLEA ALLERGY. GO TO VET

SARCOPTIC HEAD MANGE. GO TO VET

RINGWORM. GO TO VET

Fleas

Even if only one flea takes a liking to your dog and "moves in," its presence may cause wisespread allergic skin irritation. Moreover, the ubiquitous flea is part of the life cycle of the tapeworm, so apart from his external problems with fleas, your dog may develop internal parasites as well.

Although your dog's fleas are called *dog fleas,* if a dog is not available they'll make do with another host, and that other host may be you! It's not always appreciated that fleas spend a lot of time *off* the dog anyway and they'll snuggle happily into carpets, baseboards, bedding and so on. So you'll have to de-flea not only the dog but his environment, too.

You may sometimes see fleas (brownish, jumping creatures) running around a light-colored dog or, more easily, spot their feces (black specks) in the fur. They often congregate round the head and ears, on the back of the neck, base of tail and the tail itself. To deter them, dust the dog with flea powder or spray him with an aerosol (if necessary, use a strong brand if your vet approves). Start at the dog's extremities and work the powder towards his middle, so forcing the fleas to retreat. Brush out the powder onto newspaper and burn this immediately. Continue this procedure at weekly intervals until there is no sign of fleas — and repeat regularly to prevent their moving back in! Flea collars are another preventative that you might try, although not everyone is convinced that they work.

SWELLINGS

Patches confined to inside of rear legs and along abdomen or on flanks?

OR

Baldness over elbow joints, skin brownish-grey and wrinkled, condition slow to develop?

OR

Patches confined to area surrounding collar?

Small pimple-like swellings accompanied by scratching?

Probably HORMONAL IMBALANCE. GO TO VET

CALLUS from dog lying with weight on elbows. Provide soft mat for dog to lie on and massage the affected areas with petroleum jelly

May be due to rubbing from collar. Leave off when indoors

Probably INSECT BITES. See page 42 and GO TO VET if necessary. A singular, painful swelling on or just under the skin may be an ABSCESS, which needs veterinary attention

The genitals

These two pages deal only with abnormalities occuring in the female dog's genital system. As the male dog's genital and urinary systems are so closely bound together, refer to page 32, *The Waterworks,* for your male pet's "personal problems." Give your female a check for breast tumors every three months by rolling her onto her back and feeling for any hard lumps in the breast tissue. If you find some, see the vet at once, as they may spread quickly. The average female will come into season ("heat") twice each year, usually in late winter and again in the summer, but variations in timing are very common, and it is not unusual for a female to come into season only once a year. Females do not experience a menopause but the frequency or intensity of "heats" will probably diminish with age.

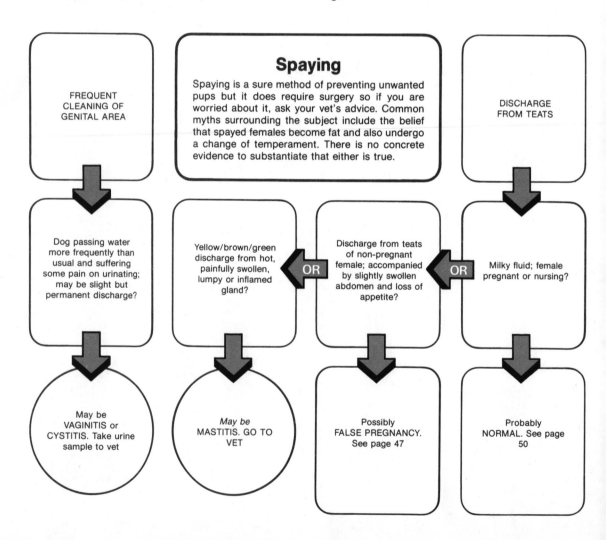

FREQUENT CLEANING OF GENITAL AREA

Spaying

Spaying is a sure method of preventing unwanted pups but it does require surgery so if you are worried about it, ask your vet's advice. Common myths surrounding the subject include the belief that spayed females become fat and also undergo a change of temperament. There is no concrete evidence to substantiate that either is true.

DISCHARGE FROM TEATS

Dog passing water more frequently than usual and suffering some pain on urinating; may be slight but permanent discharge?

Yellow/brown/green discharge from hot, painfully swollen, lumpy or inflamed gland?

OR

Discharge from teats of non-pregnant female; accompanied by slightly swollen abdomen and loss of appetite?

OR

Milky fluid; female pregnant or nursing?

May be VAGINITIS or CYSTITIS. Take urine sample to vet

May be MASTITIS. GO TO VET

Possibly FALSE PREGNANCY. See page 47

Probably NORMAL. See page 50

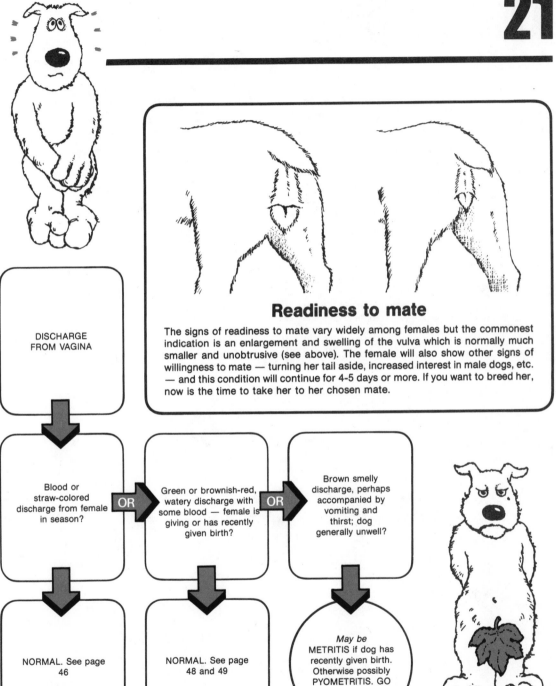

Readiness to mate

The signs of readiness to mate vary widely among females but the commonest indication is an enlargement and swelling of the vulva which is normally much smaller and unobtrusive (see above). The female will also show other signs of willingness to mate — turning her tail aside, increased interest in male dogs, etc. — and this condition will continue for 4-5 days or more. If you want to breed her, now is the time to take her to her chosen mate.

DISCHARGE FROM VAGINA

Blood or straw-colored discharge from female in season?

OR

Green or brownish-red, watery discharge with some blood — female is giving or has recently given birth?

OR

Brown smelly discharge, perhaps accompanied by vomiting and thirst; dog generally unwell?

NORMAL. See page 46

NORMAL. See page 48 and 49

May be METRITIS if dog has recently given birth. Otherwise possibly PYOMETRITIS. GO TO VET in all cases

The limbs

The most usual reason for problems with your dog's muscles and bone structure will come as the result of some accident, injury or external factor — such as being hit by a car — so if he develops *sudden* lameness in one or more legs or any other unusual movement, it's prudent to get the vet to check him over. Fractures and dislocations which happen as the result of accidents are dealt with more fully on page 41 in the first-aid section of the book.

Removing a foreign body

Pull the foreign body out with tweezers and bathe any remaining small wound with a suitable antiseptic obtained from the vet or a pet shop. If the object is deeply imbedded or you can feel but not see it clearly, go to the vet. If the dog has picked up a stone from a newly tarred road, scrape off as much tar as you can and then rub the pad gently with butter to remove the rest.

GRADUAL ONSET OF LAMENESS IN ONE OR MORE LEGS

LAMENESS IN ONE FOOT OR LEG ONLY

Older animal?

OR

Progressive lameness coupled with uneven gait in large breed — one or both hindlegs may be affected?

OR

Young dog; limbs are bowed and joints swollen?

Nails too long or broken?

May be ARTHRITIS. GO TO VET FOR DIAGNOSIS

Possibly HIP DYSPLASIA. GO TO VET

Could be RICKETS. GO TO VET FOR ADVICE and alter diet to include more calcium, Vitamin D, and phosphorus

Clip claws carefully (see panel)

Pedicures

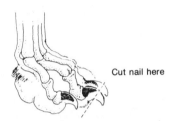

Cut nail here

If your dog's claws need clipping, use ordinary human nail clippers or special animal ones from a pet shop and cut the nail in front of the quick (see diagram). If you cut through the quick itself, it will bleed and almost certainly hurt your pet. The bleeding should eventually stop, but you can hurry it up by dabbing the claw with flour or drawing a styptic pencil across the remaining nail. Don't be surprised if the dog is less likely to be enthusiastic about future claw-clipping exercises after this!

Paralysis

Paralysis can occur in a variety of situations and is not always the result of an accident – although normally, healthy dogs are unlikely to suffer from paralysis without some external cause. In any event, the condition is very serious and requires immediate veterinary attention. There is not a lot you can do by way of first aid, but you can help the dog by following the advice given on page 42.

OTHER UNUSUAL MOVEMENT OF BODY

PARALYSIS

OR

Foreign body or minor cut in pad?

Toy breed (ie miniature poodle); leg frequently carried off ground?

OR

Dog is reluctant to move, turns whole body, rather than flexing spine, and suffers pain on doing so?

Onset maybe sudden and may affect part or whole of body?

Remove foreign body or dress wound (see panel and page 34)

Probably RECURRENT DISLOCATION OF KNEE CAP. CHECK WITH VET

Possibly SLIPPED DISC or STRAIN. GO TO VET

GO TO VET IMMEDIATELY FOR DIAGNOSIS (see also page 42)

The mouth and teeth

Check over your dog's mouth and teeth regularly, and if you clean his teeth occasionally, using a clean cloth moistened in saltwater, it will help prevent tartar from building up. Chewable toys, like the "bones" and "chews" made of processed hide available from a pet shop, will also keep his teeth and gums in good condition, as will the occasional feeding of coarsely cut raw meat. Damaged or loose teeth should receive veterinary attention as soon as possible, al-

though they don't normally pose a serious problem. Bleeding gums or bright red edging where the gums meet the teeth are usually an indication of gum disease (often caused by tartar) and should be checked to prevent the complaint from spreading.

Cleaning the teeth

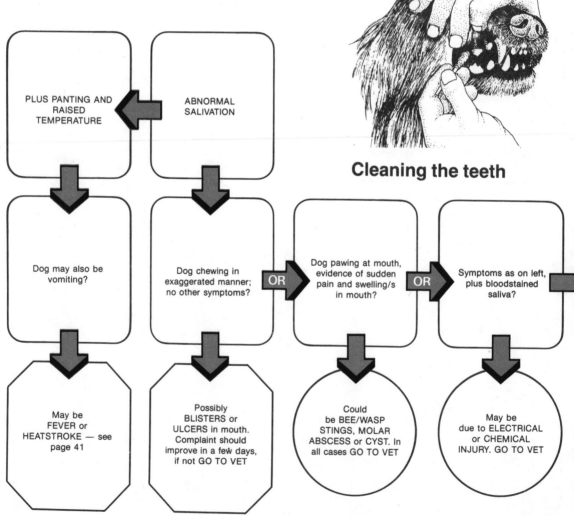

| PLUS PANTING AND RAISED TEMPERATURE | ← | ABNORMAL SALIVATION |

| Dog may also be vomiting? | Dog chewing in exaggerated manner; no other symptoms? | OR | Dog pawing at mouth, evidence of sudden pain and swelling/s in mouth? | OR | Symptoms as on left, plus bloodstained saliva? |

May be FEVER or HEATSTROKE — see page 41

Possibly BLISTERS or ULCERS in mouth. Complaint should improve in a few days, if not GO TO VET

Could be BEE/WASP STINGS, MOLAR ABSCESS or CYST. In all cases GO TO VET

May be due to ELECTRICAL or CHEMICAL INJURY. GO TO VET

WARNING
Excessive salivation coupled with any or all of the following — high temperature, dilated pupils, snapping and biting at objects for no apparent reason, no sensitivity to pain, paralysis or convulsions — may be an indication of rabies. See page 45 and contact either your vet or the public health officer immediately.

Removing a foreign body

If your dog suddenly starts pawing at his mouth and salivating, but presents no other symptoms, he may have a foreign body stuck between his teeth (i.e., a bone or wood splinter). If this is the case, steady his head while keeping his mouth open and try to push the object loose with a clean cocktail stick or your finger. When something is lodged between the back teeth and roof of the mouth, try to flick it free with a teaspoon handle. Anything that remains persistently stuck or is very far back in throat needs the vet's attention.

GUM INFLAMMATION

SWOLLEN TONSILS AND LYMPH GLANDS AT BASE OF JAW

 OR

Bad breath, wet, greasy and reddened skin in folds at corner of mouth (especially in breeds such as spaniels with loose, floppy mouths)?

Whole of mouth and tongue inflamed — dog may refuse food?

OR

Reddened gums plus red tip to tongue?

Dog may be coughing, listless, off food and possibly running a temperature?

LABIAL ECZEMA. If mild, wash night and morning with dilute, lukewarm antiseptic, cleaning and drying between folds. Apply antiseptic cream around lips. Severe cases need veterinary attention

Bathe with 50/50 solution of glycerine and water. Give soft minced foods mixed with pinch of salt. GO TO VET if complaint does not clear

Could be GINGIVITIS. May not be serious but should receive veterinary attention

TONSILLITIS. GO TO VET

The nose

A dog's nose should always be clean, and any secretions should be clear and watery. A sticky, cloudy, yellowish or greenish discharge is abnormal and should be investigated. The nose should be cold to the touch but don't rely on it for too exact a guide to the dog's temperature, good health or sickness. If you suspect that the dog has something stuck in its nose, go to the vet — such things are not easy to remove at home, and any attempt to do so may do more harm than good.

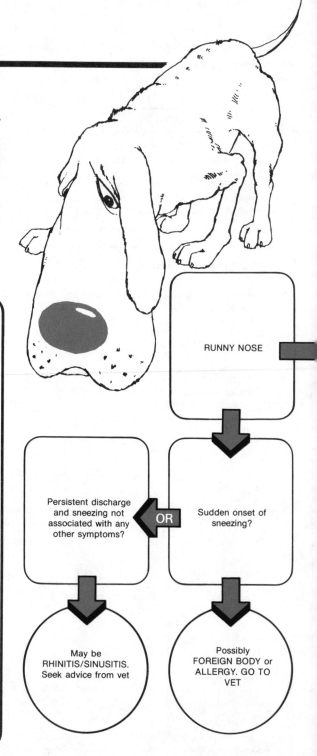

RUNNY NOSE

Sudden onset of sneezing?

Persistent discharge and sneezing not associated with any other symptoms?

OR

May be RHINITIS/SINUSITIS. Seek advice from vet

Possibly FOREIGN BODY or ALLERGY. GO TO VET

Applying nosedrops

Tip the dog's head back so his nose points upwards and he can't see what you are doing. Apply several nosedrops to the nostrils, but don't touch the nose itself with the dropper. The drops will work their way in with gravity and the natural breathing motions. If the animal develops a nose bleed, put a cold compress on the top and sides of the nose and press hard. You can also try putting damp bits of gauze into the nostrils, but the dog is unlikely to cooperate. If the bleeding recurs or is abnormally profuse or prolonged, check with the vet.

The importance of smell

All members of the dog family have a highly developed sense of smell which plays an important role in both their hunting and social activities — it is a means of communication between the sexes and, also, between packs in the wild. Although the domestic dog no longer requires such a heightened sense of smell in order to hunt efficiently, he still uses his nose to glean information about the where-abouts of other dogs, mainly by smelling their feces or urine, which contain special secretions individual to each dog, a fact that you'll doubtless notice when taking him out for walks!

The dog's sense of smell has also been cultivated by man for his own ends. For many years they have been used to retrieve game for hunting parties, in rescue operations (the St. Bernard springs instantly to mind), and more recently as tracker dogs by police hot on the heels of escaped criminals or hidden drugs.

PLUS DISCHARGE FROM EYES AND HIGH TEMPERATURE

If this combination of symptoms occurs, the dog requires immediate veterinary attention. Do not wait for temperature to return to normal.

REMEMBER

Many of the problems affecting your dog's nasal system may, in fact, stem from an illness or infection of his chest and respiratory system The three are closely interlinked so take a look at the following pages 28-29 covering these problems too

The respiratory system

The average dog breaths about 30-50 times a minute. After exercise or excitement and on warm days, he naturally breaths much faster — and when his chest or respiratory system is affected, your dog's breathing will be different, too. Sneezing or even pawing at the nose is seldom an indication of anything serious unless it is persistent and causing the dog distress. Minor irritations such as dust or pollen may cause your dog to sneeze — perhaps for quite some time — but won't be a problem unless an allergic reaction results. If, however, you think your dog looks generally unwell, check with the vet, as many respiratory complaints are highly contagious. Kennel cough, in particular, is most commonly found in dogs which have spent some time in kennels (hence its common name).

The lungs

Dogs are generally healthy creatures and normally have a particularly robust respiratory system. Complaints in this area are few and far between but, when they do occur, must not be taken lightly, as they will quickly become worse if immediate treatment is not given. You should learn to recognize your dog's normal breathing so you will be alert to any abnormality. Some pedigreed breeds are especially prone to respiratory problems — notably the short-nosed breeds such as pugs and bulldogs. It's worth bearing this in mind if you're considering such a purchase.

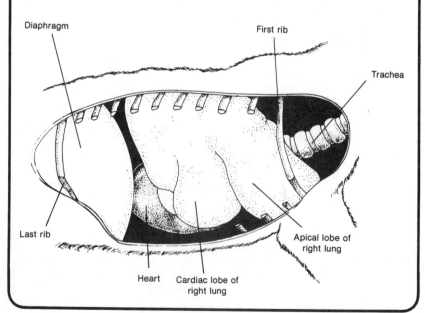

Diaphragm

First rib

Trachea

Last rib

Apical lobe of right lung

Heart   Cardiac lobe of right lung

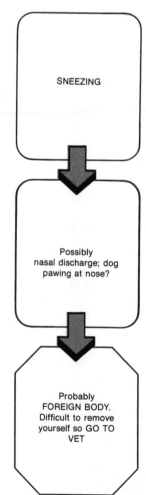

SNEEZING

Possibly nasal discharge; dog pawing at nose?

Probably FOREIGN BODY. Difficult to remove yourself so GO TO VET

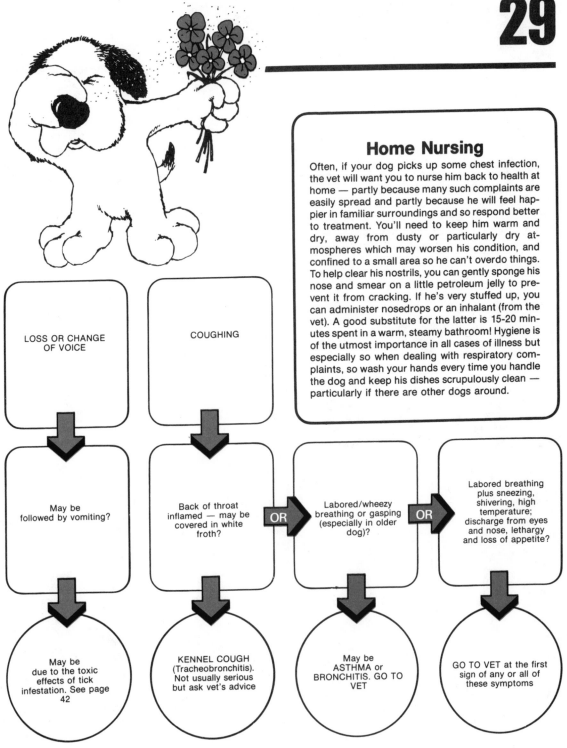

Home Nursing

Often, if your dog picks up some chest infection, the vet will want you to nurse him back to health at home — partly because many such complaints are easily spread and partly because he will feel happier in familiar surroundings and so respond better to treatment. You'll need to keep him warm and dry, away from dusty or particularly dry atmospheres which may worsen his condition, and confined to a small area so he can't overdo things. To help clear his nostrils, you can gently sponge his nose and smear on a little petroleum jelly to prevent it from cracking. If he's very stuffed up, you can administer nosedrops or an inhalant (from the vet). A good substitute for the latter is 15-20 minutes spent in a warm, steamy bathroom! Hygiene is of the utmost importance in all cases of illness but especially so when dealing with respiratory complaints, so wash your hands every time you handle the dog and keep his dishes scrupulously clean — particularly if there are other dogs around.

LOSS OR CHANGE OF VOICE

COUGHING

May be followed by vomiting?

Back of throat inflamed — may be covered in white froth?

OR

Labored/wheezy breathing or gasping (especially in older dog)?

OR

Labored breathing plus sneezing, shivering, high temperature; discharge from eyes and nose, lethargy and loss of appetite?

May be due to the toxic effects of tick infestation. See page 42

KENNEL COUGH (Tracheobronchitis). Not usually serious but ask vet's advice

May be ASTHMA or BRONCHITIS. GO TO VET

GO TO VET at the first sign of any or all of these symptoms

The stomach

Many dogs will vomit occasionally in the normal course of events, especially if they've been scavenging, and won't suffer any ill effects. Don't worry if your young dog is sick once in a while either — he's probably just been exploring what's edible and what's not! Dietary disorders are often the cause of stomach trouble, and although most dogs adore bones, they are often the cause of such complaints — constipation and intestinal blockage in particular.

However, if any symptom persists for more than a few hours, is accompanied by deep malaise or weakness in the dog, or there is evidence of blood in stools or vomit go to the vet at once. Also remember to treat the dog for dehydration if necessary (see page 36). BEWARE that some very severe cases of diarrhea, accompanied by straining, can easily be mistaken for constipation. If you suspect this GO TO THE VET IMMEDIATELY.

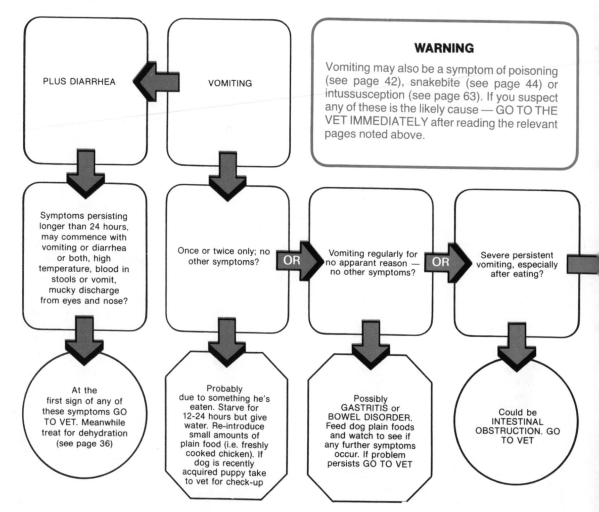

PLUS DIARRHEA

VOMITING

WARNING

Vomiting may also be a symptom of poisoning (see page 42), snakebite (see page 44) or intussusception (see page 63). If you suspect any of these is the likely cause — GO TO THE VET IMMEDIATELY after reading the relevant pages noted above.

Symptoms persisting longer than 24 hours, may commence with vomiting or diarrhea or both, high temperature, blood in stools or vomit, mucky discharge from eyes and nose?

Once or twice only; no other symptoms?

OR

Vomiting regularly for no apparant reason — no other symptoms?

OR

Severe persistent vomiting, especially after eating?

At the first sign of any of these symptoms GO TO VET. Meanwhile treat for dehydration (see page 36)

Probably due to something he's eaten. Starve for 12-24 hours but give water. Re-introduce small amounts of plain food (i.e. freshly cooked chicken). If dog is recently acquired puppy take to vet for check-up

Possibly GASTRITIS or BOWEL DISORDER. Feed dog plain foods and watch to see if any further symptoms occur. If problem persists GO TO VET

Could be INTESTINAL OBSTRUCTION. GO TO VET

Internal parasites

Many parasites spend part of their lives in the dog's intestines and can be present with or without causing illness. If you think the dog may have parasites or you have acquired a new puppy, take a sample of his feces to the vet for analysis. Apart from the necessity of eradicating them for the well-being of the dog, some parasites, such as roundworms, can also become a human health hazard. Some tapeworms are carried by external parasites, such as the flea, and others can be picked up by the dog's eating raw meat or catching his own prey. So if your dog is infested with fleas, start checking his stools for small white objects that look rather like cooked rice — they are in fact pieces of worm. Hookworms are a problem in warm climates, as are protozoan *coccidia,* and both require intensive treatment if they are to be eradicated. Make sure all puppies are wormed at an early age (see page 50).

CONSTIPATION

DIARRHEA

OR

Abnormal thirst in female, possibly accompanied by vaginal discharge?

OR

Dog may be straining to pass stools with little or no success, and suffering obvious pain on doing so?

Hard, dry stools produced with difficulty?

Condition lasts no longer than 24 hours, stools normal color, no other symptoms?

May be PYOMETRITIS. GO TO VET

A variety of complaints will give rise to these symptoms, all of which require veterinary attention

May be due to incorrect diet. Decrease protein and increase biscuit, bran or meal content. Alternatively try a laxative; e.g. liquid paraffin. If dog seems in pain GO TO VET

Probably due to over-rich diet (e.g., all meat) or scavenging. Starve for 12-24 hours but give water. Resume feeding with plain foods. If dog is recently acquired puppy, GO TO VET for check-up

The waterworks

This section covers the urinary systems of both sexes, plus the genital system of the male dog. You can prevent many problems from occurring in this area by making sure your dog always has plenty of fresh water to drink and a fair proportion of his diet is made up of moist food. Never withhold water from him if he has urinary problems. Basically, when and wherever you notice something wrong or out of the ordinary with your dog's waterworks, call the vet.

Health and dry food

A good diet is a great help in regulating your dog's waterworks. Lots of fresh water should be available at all times, and remember that a pinch of table salt in the dog's food markedly increases his water intake. With dry food diets *never* leave him without adequate water.

Incontinence

This is usually a problem with an old or sick dog and should not be confused with the situation where an animal has *had* to "go" indoors even though he has control over his bladder. Rather, incontinence is the unconscious passing of urine. See if the vet can do something about it, but never restrict the dog's water intake, as this will distress him. If sores appear on his body through the frequent passing of urine, make sure he lies on plenty of absorbent bedding (such as a pile of old towels) and spread a thin layer of petroleum jelly over the area of skin usually wetted by the urine.

A further problem with older dogs may result from a chronic form of nephritis. Animals with this complaint often lose their appetites and develop a severe thirst. Unlike dogs with ordinary nephritis, they may pass large quantities of pale urine and rapidly lose weight. Incontinence may also result from damaged kidneys.

Start house-training your puppy at an early age — when they reach 6 weeks old is about the right time — as the longer you leave it, the more difficult it will become. Be patient and don't lose your temper if he has an accident indoors. For further details on toilet training see page 56.

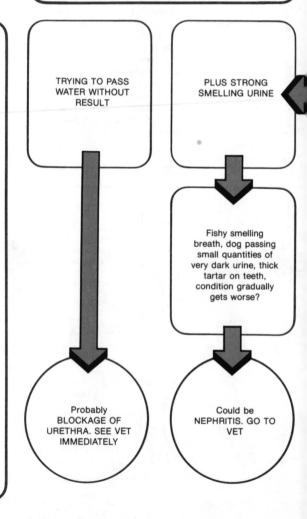

TRYING TO PASS WATER WITHOUT RESULT

PLUS STRONG SMELLING URINE

Fishy smelling breath, dog passing small quantities of very dark urine, thick tartar on teeth, condition gradually gets worse?

Probably BLOCKAGE OF URETHRA. SEE VET IMMEDIATELY

Could be NEPHRITIS. GO TO VET

Taking a urine sample

Urine samples are invaluable for the vet in diagnosing all sorts of ailments. The best sample for diagnosis is one taken in the early morning, and collecting a small sample (which is all the vet will require) is, happily, relatively easy. Put the dog on his leash and go out with him, taking with you a jar with a lid. When the dog urinates, slip the jar into the flow and catch a little of the urine.

Leg cocking

Male dogs indicate their territory by cocking their legs every few yards or so and marking the spot with urine (females don't cock their legs, but squat instead). Both sexes instinctively try to cover their droppings with earth, after the custom of their wild ancestors, but most domestic dogs merely indicate their intentions by a little theatrical scratching with the hind feet in the general area of the droppings. They seldom make anywhere near as good a job of it as a cat does!

PASSING WATER MORE FREQUENTLY THAN USUAL

Passing small amounts of urine which may be cloudy or bloodstained? Dog straining and in pain after urinating?

OR

Passing water in bursts rather than even flow; may be evidence of blood in urine?

OR

Severe thirst, lots of weak, pale urine, no other symptoms; dog fat and happy?

OR

Severe thirst, sickly-sweet smelling breath, animal generally unwell — passing large amounts of urine, losing weight?

Probably
CYSTITIS or STONES BLOCKING URETHRA. GO TO VET

Possibly
ENLARGED PROSTATE GLAND. GO TO VET

May be
WATER DIABETES, although this is rare in dogs. GO TO VET

Probably
SUGAR DIABETES. GO TO VET

Caring for your patient

The first thing you must realize is that an injured or sick dog is in pain and will probably be afraid. He may often feel that his master (who has perhaps unintentionally aggravated the injury) can't be trusted any more, and his natural tendency will be to run away and hide, which is obviously not very useful if he needs treatment!

Handling a sick (or bad tempered) dog

1 Go up to the dog in a firm, but kind and quiet way. Use his name a lot if you know it, and in any case, talk gently to him. Let him sniff the back of your closed fist (an open hand may make him think you are going to hit him).
2 Do nothing to injure him further.
3 Restrain the dog by wrapping him securely in a blanket or other suitable material so he won't injure himself any more — nor be able to bite or claw you. Protect yourself, if necessary, with heavy gloves.
4 If you can get the dog in a situation different from the norm, say on a tabletop instead of the ground, this will make him a little uncertain and therefore more tractable.

Muzzles

Many dogs won't need a muzzle, but if you have to handle a strange or injured dog, it's not a bad idea to use one (follow diagrams below).

Bandages

Wounds usually heal best when left uncovered, but there are times when they need a bandage — when they are getting dirty and infected, for example, or if the patient is licking them and so preventing them from healing.

Bandages should not interfere with the dog's circulation, so you must make the loops firm but not tight. You'll need a helper to restrain the patient while you fix the bandage.

Foot

Bathe and cleanse the cut and pad with cotton, especially between the toes to prevent irritation. Roll the bandage from the bottom of the foot upwards around the leg. Fix with adhesive tape to prevent it from slipping down. It's rather better to sew the ends rather than leave them loose to be nibbled or gnawed. A child's or doll's sock will make a good light bandage. Never fix anything with a rubber band, as this may cut into the leg and cause further damage.

Head

Give the bandage two turns around the neck, taking it over the head, down side of face, under jaw and around the neck again. Fix at back of neck. Will not slip if stitched at several points with thread.

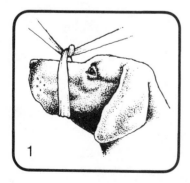
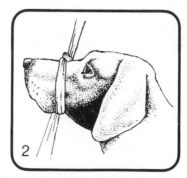
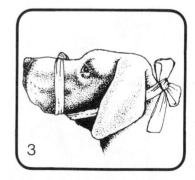

Taking the pulse

A dog's pulse is easiest to take on the large artery running down the inside of the hind leg. Feel for it with your index and middle fingers just below the point where the leg joins the body. A normal dog's pulse is between 80-140 a minute. Faster is a characteristic of shock or fever, while a weak or almost non-existent pulse needs immediate veterinary attention.

Administering pills

Many dogs are masters at the art of pill-detection, even when one is crushed and mixed with their usual food. Although the vet will try to give you drugs made as attractive as possible to animals, often your dog will take a bite and spit it out. The best way of making sure the pill goes down is to administer it yourself. Hold the pill between the index and middle finger of your right hand. Put the thumb of your other hand behind the dog's large upper fang tooth and press up on the roof of the mouth. At the same time, press down on his lower jaw with your right thumb, push the pill far down his throat, close the mouth and tap the dog briskly under the chin. The dog will usually be startled by all this and will swallow the pill.

Chest

Place layers of bandage over nape of neck, across chest and between front legs. Finish with tight knot at back or stitch ends.

Abdomen — many-tailed bandage

Make from rectangle or square of clean cloth and knot over back. If necessary, gauze or padding can be placed between wound and bandage.

Taking a temperature

You should take a dog's temperature rectally, so use a proper rectal thermometer (not an oral one, as the mecury bulb can easily break). Shake the thermometer until the column of mercury is just above the bulb (about 96°F, 36°C). Get someone to hold the dog on a table gently but firmly. Lubricate the thermometer with soap or petroleum jelly and insert it into the dog's anus with a gentle twisting movement until about half the length is inside. Remove after about 3 minutes, wipe with cotton and read. The average dog's temperature is between 100-103°F (most about 101.5°F), or 38° to 39°C.

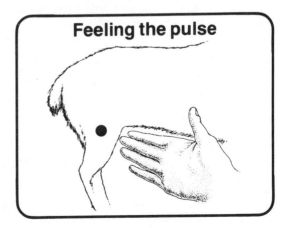

Feeling the pulse

Difficult dogs will have to be given a pill by the vet and, when at all possible, the vet will give the drug by means of an injection. If your dog is exceptionally nervous, ask the vet if you should tranquilize him before coming to the office — and, if so, with what? Never give the dog any drug which hasn't been prescribed for that particular dog at that particular time, and never use up old drugs.

Liquids

To give a dog a liquid potion, don't use a spoon. Put the right amount of medicine into a small bottle. Pull out the corner of the dog's lip to make a "pocket" and pour the medicine in, a little at a time. Don't raise his nose too much or the liquid may cause the animal to choke.

Force-feeding

If a sick dog *really* will not eat, sometimes you may have to force-feed him. Even more vital, you must replace lost fluids by feeding him liquid in the same way as you'd administer liquid medicine (see above), as this helps prevent dehydration. Glucose mixed with boiled, cooled water is an ideal liquid to give, but not milk.

If you are nursing a convalescent dog (not one that's dehydrated), the easiest way of force-feeding is to make the food liquid enough to feed as fluid. If a sick dog has a temperature, he should not be fed solid food anyway, but even when the temperature is normal, it is easiest to give several small meals rather than one or two large ones. Give a little at each feed, or the dog may vomit it up again (a few teaspoons of food every 2 or 3 hours is about right). You should also measure the fluid intake and make sure the dog gets about 1 tablespoon of liquid/water per 10 lbs. or so of its own weight per hour. You can use milk to form part of this allowance, as long as it doesn't cause diarrhea and the dog is not dehydrated.

Dehydration

Loss of body fluids and salt is much more dangerous to any dog than lack of food, so if you suspect your dog is dehydrated through either vomiting or diarrhea, give him frequent small doses of glucose and water, salt and water or just plain water. If he cannot drink for himself, spoon or squirt the liquid into his mouth with a syringe (without the needle, of course). Don't use milk or brandy, but half a teaspoonful of milk of magnesia could help if he is vomiting. With diarrhea, concentrate on water replacement, and you can try human kaolin and morphine diarrhea mixtures, as these are sometimes a great help.

It is vital that the dog doesn't get seriously dehydrated. Signs are decreased elasticity of the skin, so pick up a fold of skin from the middle of his back — the skin should spring immediately back into place. Any sluggishness or tent-like appearance means the dog is dehydrated. Other signs are drying of the mucus membrane lining the mouth and eyes, sunken eyes and some appearance of shock (see page 44). If you notice any of these signs, you should get to the vet at once. Meanwhile treat the dog as outlined above.

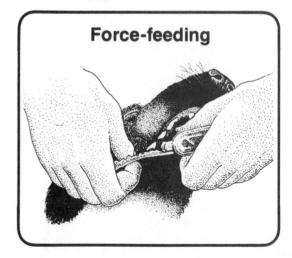

Force-feeding

Nursing a sick dog

Like any human patient, a sick dog needs careful nursing to help him get better, but try not to fuss over him too much. Sleep is vital, and he should be left in a quiet atmosphere with lowered lighting. Give the dog a comfortable bed out of the way of drafts (especially at his eye level), and a good arrangement is to provide him with a chest or box with one open end, as illustrated. Make the bed cozy with old blankets and newspapers, and change these when they get soiled. Keep the dog warm (in a temperature of at least 60°F, 16°C) with a well-covered hot water bottle (kept hot), or a heating pad (again well-covered so the dog can't burn himself).

If the weather is not too bad, and the dog not too sick, you could let him out of doors to relieve himself, but always keep him on a leash and wearing a coat. If possible, you should try to arrange out-of-door toilet use. Not only is this more pleasant for you, but a house-trained dog may suffer mentally if he has to relieve himself indoors. If he *can't* go out, you'll have to protect the floor of the room with thick layers of newspaper laid on top of old vinyl floor covering. Clean the room and bed frequently, remove any excreta at once and, if possible, groom the dog daily.

Newspapers or blankets provide suitable bedding but only use blankets if the dog is clean. In any case they should be covered by an easily washable sheet. If the dog is incontinent, put newspapers under his rear end to keep the bed dry, and cotton between his thighs and under the tail. Sponge with weak antiseptic and warm water several times a day, and sprinkle his rear end and abdomen with talc. Use zinc ointment in the same way if the dog has diarrhea.

Change the dog's drinking water frequently and, if the vet approves, offer him some of his favorite tidbits to tempt him to eat. You may have to force-feed (see opposite) if he simply refuses to eat. If necessary, bathe the dog's eyes and nose with warm salt water, and if the skin on the nose gets cracked, a little cod-liver oil smoothed on should help.

A very sick dog is best confined to one room or a small area, but when he is a bit better, you can let him wander freely around the house if the vet approves. Most really sick dogs will be hospitalized by the vet, but some degree of the "intensive care" outlined in the previous pages may sometimes be necessary.

The convalescent

First aid for your dog

The next few pages deal with first aid in emergency and non-emergency situations — you should always try to distinguish between the two. Try to keep calm so you can assess whether you need the vet right away or whether your first-aid treatment is adequate for the time being and you can see the vet in the morning — or even not at all. If you can, practice as many of the first-aid procedures as possible to become familiar with them should you ever need to use them for real.

Emergency procedure

As far as possible, start first-aid treatment *while on your way to the vet.* For example, if you are trying to control bleeding, start at once, but meanwhile, get the dog into the car and get someone to drive you to the vet. Continue the treatment while you are traveling there. If there is no possible way you can get to the vet quickly and safely, get someone to phone for him while you carry on with the first-aid treatment.

The following are always emergencies:
● Bleeding you cannot control (opposite)
● Breathing difficulties — when a dog is having extreme difficulty in breathing after an accident, heart attack or when unconscious (see opposite page)
● Burns (see page 40)
● Collapse (see page 40)
● Convulsions (see page 40)
● Eyeball, injury to (see page 40)
● Fractures or dislocations (see page 41)
● Paralysis (page 42)
● Poisoning (page 43)
● Rabies (page 44)
● Shock (see page 44)
● Snakebite (page 44)

Other common problems needing first aid are injury by fishhooks and insect bites. The conditions are dealt with in alphabetical order to facilitate ease of reference, and a section on serious diseases can be found on page 45.

Bleeding

If bleeding doesn't stop within 5 minutes, you must try to staunch the flow using the following procedure:

1 With a clean cloth, or even your hand, apply direct pressure to the wound. If blood seeps through, apply more bandage or gauze pad on top of old — don't try to remove old bandage.
2 If such pressure won't stop the bleeding, find the nearest pressure point (see diagram) and compress the artery against its underlying bone. Use the flat part of your fingers — not your thumb or finger tips.
3 As a last resort you can try a tourniquet, although this carries the greater risk of stopping circulation to the affected part and causing gangrene. Use it only to save life when nothing else is working, and release intermittently.

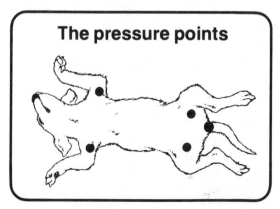

The pressure points

Breathing difficulties

Many things may cause a dog to have difficulty in breathing — perhaps obstruction of the air passage to the lungs by a foreign body or the dog's own tongue if he is unconscious, strangulation by his collar, electrocution, drowning, heart attack or chest injuries. If the dog is breathing with difficulty, clear airway and, if necessary, start artificial respiration immediately. If you cannot *see* breathing movement place your ear on the dog's chest and listen for a heartbeat or take his pulse (see page 35). If the heart has stopped within the last minute or so, but you think the dog is not yet dead, apply heart massage and artificial respiration together. Never attempt the kiss of life if you have reason to believe that poison is involved (see page 43).

Artificial respiration

1 Open dog's mouth, grasp tongue and pull it well forward and clear of back of throat. Wipe away any mucus or blood. Check for any obstruction.
2 Remove any collar or constricting item.
3 If the animal has fluid in its throat or is a victim of drowning, hold it upside down by its rear legs for 15-30 seconds.
4 If the dog is still not breathing properly, start artificial respiration. Close mouth, place your mouth over his nose and exhale to force air through his nose to the lungs. Watch the dog's chest for the lungs to inflate. Remove your mouth, and repeat the cycle about six times a minute. You may need to carry on for 30-60 minutes, until the dog is breathing by itself or is pronounced dead.

Heart massage/compression

If you cannot hear the dog's heartbeat, strike his chest sharply with your fist once or twice in the region just behind his left elbow. If heart is still not going, apply heart massage. Place the dog on its right side on a firm surface. Put the fingers of one hand on each side of the chest over the heart area and compress it *firmly,* but not too hard. Then release the pressure. Repeat 70 times a minute.

Applying a tourniquet

First aid for your dog

Burns

Animals are afraid of fire, so burns from an open flame are not too common, although a dog dozing by the fire may get singed or burnt. He can burn his feet, though, by walking on a hot surface, and scalds are quite common. Puppies, especially, might chew on electric wire, which will cause a special type of burn, and this will often be accompanied by electric shock.

Heat Burns

1 Do not apply butter, grease or any ointment.
2 Soak a cloth in cold water and hold to burned place.
3 Send for the vet if the burn seems serious. A superficial burn is painful, reddens the skin and singes the hair, but the latter will not pull out easily. A serious burn is actually less painful because the nerves have been destroyed. The skin may be white, black or brown, and the hair will either be gone completely or will pull out easily.
4 Keep the burn covered with wet dressings covered with thick, dry towels.
5 Make the dog stay lying down, restrained in warm blankets.
6 Give fluid as for dehydration, unless the dog is vomiting.
7 Treat for shock (see page 44).

Chemical burns

1 Wash burned area with lots of plain water, especially if around face.
2 If acid, rinse with solution of 1 teaspoon bicarbonate of soda to 1 quart of water. If alkali, use plain water only.
3 Apply soothing ointment, e.g., olive oil.
4 You should, of course muzzle and restrain the dog before treatment.

Collapse

In this situation apply common-sense first aid while getting to the vet as quickly as possible.

1 Check pulse, pupils, breathing and temperature. Apply artificial respiration and/or heart massage as outlined on previous pages.
2 Always handle your dog as if he may have a broken bone or other serious internal injury.
3 Treat for shock (see page 44).

Convulsion/fits

There are basically two kinds of convulsions — the single convulsion which lasts for a minute or two and doesn't recur for at least 24 hours, and repeated or continuous convulsions, which are serious emergencies and need veterinary attention immediately. In the latter situation, you should gently restrain the dog by placing a towel over him so he can't injure himself. Don't put your hand on the dog or in or near his mouth, as you may get bitten and will require treatment yourself. Once you've restrained the dog, get to the vet immediately. Single convulsions also require veterinary attention but are usually not so serious. Again, restrain the animal and get to the vet as soon as possible.

Eyeball, injury to

If there is bleeding in the area of the eyes, apply direct pressure with dry gauze pads and go to vet. Laceration of the eyeball itself or penetration by a foreign object is very serious. Place a damp cloth over the place, and get to the vet at once. Don't try to wash the eye or remove a foreign body, or you'll undoubtedly do more harm than good. A simple bruise can usually be dealt with by a cold compress. For other eye problems, see page 16.

Fractures or dislocations

In pets these are mostly caused by car accidents or a fall. Never try to set the bone yourself, but while getting veterinary attention, you should carry out the following points:

1 Muzzle the dog.
2 Keep him on his side with the injured limb uppermost.
3 Get hold of the dog by the scruff of the neck and a fold of skin over the hips and pull him, back first, onto a blanket or board. Then you can slide him out of the way of traffic, but be careful not to place

Improvised splint

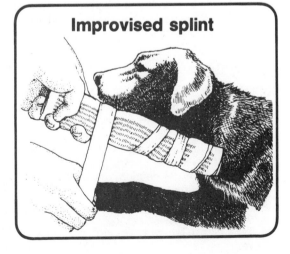

any strain on the injured leg. Otherwise, just slide the animal carefully along the ground, letting legs follow in a straight line.
4 If necessary, give artificial respiration and treat for bleeding.
5 If fragments of bone are exposed, don't try to replace them. Cover with a gauze dressing or light bandage.
6 Treat for shock (see page 44).
7 Improvise a splint from a folded newspaper, cardboard strip or a towel to support the fracture so the dog can be moved safely. Make the splint long enough to extend beyond the joints on either end of the fractured bone. Place padding between the splint and the skin, especially over the joint areas (unless the splint is made of soft material).
8 Get to the vet as soon as possible.

Heatstroke (heat exhaustion)

This often occurs if the dog is kept shut up in a house or car without shade, ventilation or water. It can also happen as a result of the dog's getting overexcited or being under stress; i.e., at dog shows. Signs are panting, slobbering, vomiting and diarrhea, raised temperature (usually above 107°F, 41.5°C) and ultimately collapse and coma.

1 Remove dog from hot spot into cool or shady area.
2 Soak dog with cold water from a hose or immerse him in an ice bath and gently massage his legs and body. Keep doing this until you reach the vet or the animal's body temperature falls to less that 103°F, 39.5°C.
3 Gently dry dog with towel. If he is conscious, give him small amounts of water. Give artificial respiration if necessary.

First aid for your dog

Insect bites and stings

Bee, wasp and hornet stings often produce large, flat, swollen weals which are both very painful and irritating, often on the head or face. If the dog is allergic to the sting, he may have developed breathing difficulties, and there is a risk of death. Fleas, sand flies, mosquitoes, ants, lice and gnat bites produce many small red pimples which are very itchy and which the dog will scratch and lick a lot. Most insect bites are just irritating or a little painful, but a bite from a poisonous spider (although rare) has far more serious effects. Luckily, there are only two poisonous spiders in the United States — the black widow and the brown recluse. If your dog gets bitten by one of these, he will require immediate veterinary attention.

and severe, possibly fatal, illness in both animals and man. If your dog shows any signs of illness after you've determined the presence of a tick, seek immediate veterinary attention. The more dangerous ticks often attach themselves to dogs around the ears, eyes and lips and may also be found between the toes and along the belly. Any found should be removed immediately, as their salivary glands may contain a strong toxic poison which is ejected into the dog's bloodstream. A meticulous search should be carried out for any others hidden between folds of the skin.

1 Remove parasite with an insecticide (flea spray). Never hold a lighted cigarette to ticks or pull them off with your fingers — instead soak them in insecticide, liquid paraffin or alcohol. After a minute or two, tease them off gently with tweezers and try to get the head out. Remove any bee sting.
2 Clean the area with soap and water, wipe with alcohol and dry. A cold compress should reduce the itching and swelling but a more severe reaction needs veterinary attention.
3 Carry out a thorough search of the dog if ticks are involved to make sure all such creatures are removed.

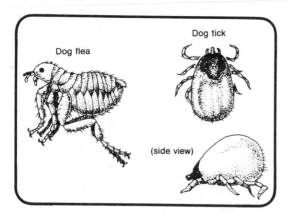

Dog tick

Dog flea

(side view)

Ticks

Ticks can also be a major problem. They should be removed as soon as they are noticed (see opposite) like brown or reddish-brown coffee-bean sized creatures with their heads embedded in the skin. Ticks are found everywhere, from densely wooded areas to your living room carpet. Among the most dangerous species in North America is the Rocky Mountain spotted fever tick, which can cause paralysis

Paralysis

Get to the vet as soon as possible. Meanwhile follow the procedure outlined below:

1 Stay calm — keep the dog quiet in a cool, dark place, and if he's only partially paralyzed, stop him from struggling.
2 Move him with caution, using a tray or blanket as a stretcher.
3 Give sedative painkillers; e.g., aspirin, if dog is conscious.
4 Take all available information on cause to vet.

Poisoning

Dogs may sometimes swallow or come into physical contact with poisons — whether from plants or chemical substances (cleaning agents, etc.). Even grass, the eating of which is normally harmless, may have been sprayed with weed-killer and have adverse effects.

Unless you catch your dog in the act, you can't always be sure that he's been poisoned, let alone know by what! However, if you find a questionable substance chewed, opened or spilled, or the dog himself is vomiting, breathing with difficulty, having abdominal pains or diarrhea, has burns or painful areas on the skin, or perhaps an unusual smell about him — act as if poison has been taken.

Blanket stretcher

1 Stop the dog from getting any more of the poison.
2 If the poison is a corrosive one (such as acid, alkali or a petroleum product like gasoline or kerosene), dilute it by giving milk or vegetable oil, but don't try to make the dog vomit. Send for the vet at once.
3 If you know for certain the poison is non-corrosive (there are traces around the mouth or on the fur), try to get the dog to vomit by giving him 1 or 2 teaspoonfuls of medical hydrogen peroxide or a strong salt or mustard solution. Get to the vet quickly, taking a sample of label or container of the poison with you if possible.
4 If you don't know what antidote to try, dilute the poison after vomiting has stopped by giving water or milk, preferably mixed with several teaspoonfuls of medical charcoal (from pharmacist).
5 If the dog is unconscious, don't give him anything by mouth, but just get to the vet promptly. Give heart massage if necessary, keeping the dog warm in a blanket and his head lowered so any fluids drain out.
6 If the dog is convulsing or very excited, don't give him anything by mouth or try to induce vomiting. Wrap him in blankets and get to the vet immediately.

First aid for your dog

Shock

"Shock" is a term used loosely and often very incorrectly. In both human and animal terms, it is much more serious than the slight feeling of malaise that might occur after a minor accident or fright, which is often called "shock." The signs of true shock in dogs are: weakness, collapse, coma, unconsciousness, pale color of mouth, lips and eyelids, coolness of skin and legs, rapid but weak pulse (may be over 140 per minute), rapid respiration (over 40 a minute), staring eyes and dilated pupils. If any or all of these signs occur after an accident or prolonged illness, treat for shock as below and call the vet immediately.

1 Keep airways open, giving artificial respiration or heart massage as necessary, bandage or splint any fracture or extensive wound.
2 Wrap the dog in a thick cloth or towel to conserve body heat. If the dog is unconscious, keep his head as low as, or lower than, the rest of the body. Gently massage legs and muscles to maintain circulation unless you suspect that they may be fractured or broken. If he is conscious and restless, keep him horizontal and well wrapped up.
3 Get to the vet's office promptly. Time is vital, especially for the intravenous introduction of fluid in severe cases.

If you *absolutely can't* get immediate veterinary help — either at all or for a few hours — give fluids orally. If the dog is conscious administer an amount (depending on dog's size) of tepid water mixed with glucose every 30 minutes for 4 to 5 doses. Don't give anything by mouth if the dog is unconscious, convulsing or vomiting. Take pulse and breathing rate every 30 minutes and record them. Note any blood in urine, etc., and report these details to the vet.

Snakebite

There are many different species of snake that might come into contact with your dog, depending on your location — ranging from a harmless garter snake to the poisonous copperhead. Not all snakebites have adverse affects on dogs, but the majority of bites are extremely painful, if not fatal. On nine out of ten occasions, you won't know which species is the cause of the trouble — or may not even be sure that your dog has been bitten by a snake at all. Symptoms range from muscular spasms to paralysis and collapse. Vomiting, exhaustion, shallow and rapid breathing, swelling and bruising are also common signs. If you suspect that your dog has been bitten, carry out the steps outlined below.

1 Do your utmost to prevent the dog from running away, since exercise spreads the venom.
2 Immobilize the dog.
3 If the snakebite is on the limb or tail, you can apply a broad, restrictive bandage (e.g., wide rubber strip) between the bite and the heart, but it must be loose enough to slip a finger underneath. This type of tourniquet will let some oxygen reach the limb but should be removed after ½ hour or when you reach the vet. If the bite is on a part of the body that cannot be constricted, simply wash the wound to remove as much venom as possible.
4 You can make linear cuts (not X-shaped) over the fang wound and apply suction with a suction cup but *never* your mouth.
5 It is essential to get to the vet as soon as possible as he may be able to administer the correct antivenin. If you can be sure of veterinary help within 30 minutes, probably the best treatment is to apply a tight tourniquet.

Serious diseases

The incidence of fatal diseases in dogs has, luckily, been drastically reduced over the last few years, thanks to improvements in vaccines, quarantine laws and increased knowledge of what they actually are and, consequently, how they can be prevented. There are basically five serious diseases that may prove fatal in dogs, but their risk of catching any of these can be greatly reduced by proper inoculation. Your veterinarian can see that your dog receives all required vaccinations, as well as annual booster shots.

Distemper

This disease is caused by a virus that can attack virtually all the dog's body tissues and so has a wide range of symptoms. It is more common in younger animals but can occur at any age, and although dogs can, and do, recover, they seldom return to normal once the virus has reached the nervous system and brain. A discharge from the eyes and nose, accompanied by coughing, vomiting and/or diarrhea and general lethargy are often the first symptoms, sometimes followed by fits, nervous twitching and finally paralysis. Distemper can also cause a hardening of the nose and pads, hence its original name "hard pad."

Canine parvovirus

This disease is an infection of the muscles controlling the heart and will cause sudden death in unvaccinated puppies. Adult dogs will appear to have severe food poisoning; i.e., vomiting and diarrhea with some evidence of internal bleeding.

Leptospirosis

There are two strains of this disease, both of which will attack the kidneys and liver, resulting in vomiting, high fever, collapse and finally coma. A noticeable yellowing of the whites of the eyes is also a symptom. One form is particularly dangerous, as it can also affect humans — known as Weil's disease.

Hepatitis

This virus is most common in pups but can affect dogs of all ages. A variety of symptoms can occur, the most common being vomiting, lack of appetite and jaundice.

Rabies

This disease is so horrible that its effects should never be underestimated. The virus can infect any warm-blooded animal — and that includes humans. Make sure your dog is properly vaccinated against rabies when he's about four months old (later than most other vaccinations). Your vet will let you know about a follow-up and booster schedule.

Rabies is usually spread when one animal bites another, but the virus can also technically enter the body through any break in the skin. Signs of infection usually develop between two weeks and two months afterwards, but it can take up to a year. Rabid dogs usually show a difference in behavior — they may become restless, extremely affectionate, terrified or shy. Some dogs hide; some develop a temperature and dilated pupils.

If you or your dog are exposed to or bitten by a rabies suspect, confine the dog, making sure you neither touch him nor get any of his saliva on you — a walking stick looped through his collar is a good "distance" control. Then give him over to a public health officer or your vet immediately. All your bite wounds should be instantly washed with lots of soap and water, and you must get to a doctor or nearest hospital at once, as injections will need to be given.

The expectant mom

Domestic dogs are fairly free with their sexual favors and as the owner of a female it's up to you to decide whether to let her breed or not. Most females come into season twice a year and, if mated, can produce an average litter of 4-8 pups. Before you let your pet breed, you should be sure that you can find good homes for her young, as far too many unwanted dogs end up in the pound where, if no one takes them, they'll have to be put to sleep. If you allow your female to breed, you should always keep one or two puppies for a short time after their birth for the physical and mental welfare of the mother.

The safest of all canine family planning — as with humans — is sterilization, but if you really feel that such an operation is necessary, ask your vet's advice, as no animal should have to undergo such an operation unless absolutely essential. Castration of the male is less frequently practiced with dogs. Dogs can go on "the pill" too, but it should only be given for limited periods and strictly under veterinary advice. A contraceptive pill (or a similar injection) will prevent the dog from coming into season but shouldn't be used as a permanent contraceptive — only if you want to prevent her from breeding for a few months for some reason.

If the female isn't spayed or on the pill, you must keep her under strict control when she is in season, or she will undoubtedly mate and have puppies. Usually a female first comes into "heat" between 6-9 months of age. If she hasn't had a "season" by 15 months, check with the vet. Male dogs, by the way, are usually sexually mature at about 6 months, but they are interested in sex all the year round, and a bunch of males will thoroughly pester a female in season!

The female in heat

Heats in females usually last from 18-21 days, although conception is only possible for a few days around the middle of the heat. The first indication that heat is starting will be a puffiness of the lips of the vulva. The bleeding starts (incidentally this is in no way comparable to human menstruation). For the next 4-14 days (on average 10), the female is extremely attractive to male dogs, but she won't have anything to do with them until the bleeding diminishes and the vulva is at its largest. This "fertile period" lasts for 5-12 days — the female is at her most fertile during the first two or three. If you want to breed her, now is the time to take her to her chosen mate — and you should allow them to mate again a couple of days later to ensure success.

Mating can take up to 10-20 minutes, and if the dogs are separated in the first two to three minutes, you can be fairly confident that conception has not taken place. If trying to separate mating dogs, do remember that there is a special "bulb" in the male's penis which locks it

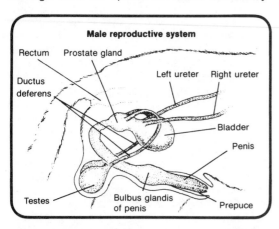

Male reproductive system

Rectum
Prostate gland
Left ureter   Right ureter
Ductus deferens
Bladder
Penis
Testes
Bulbus glandis of penis
Prepuce

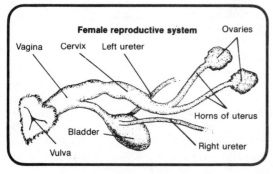

Female reproductive system

Ovaries
Vagina   Cervix   Left ureter
Horns of uterus
Bladder
Right ureter
Vulva

inside the female's vagina and withdrawal is not really possible until this bulb returns to its normal size. If, therefore, you throw a bucket of water over the pair and they drag themselves apart it may cause damage to their organs. It's far better to let the mating conclude in its own time, and then take the female to the vet within 48 hours, as he'll give her an injection which will prevent the pregnancy. This however, should not become a habit, as it might have a long-term effect on her womb.

Avoiding pregnancy

If you intend your female to have pups, don't try to have her mated at her first heat, and never mate her with a dog very much larger than herself. If you don't want her to mate, never let her out on her own, and if you take her out, make sure to keep her on a leash. Spray her rear end with a deodorant aerosol from a pet shop — and do the same to your doorstep and front gate, repeating daily. Also the vet may be able to supply some form of medication to help discourage would-be suitors. If, however, your pedigreed female gets out while in season and mates with your local neighborhood mongrel, don't think that this will spoil her chances of producing future pedigreed litters with a suitable pedigreed mate — it won't.

Pregnancy

If your female has mated without your knowledge, you will be able to tell at about 4-5 weeks that she is pregnant, as her abdomen will get noticeably larger. If you are not sure whether your female is pregnant, the vet will usually be able to tell by carefully feeling her. There are currently no blood or urine pregnancy tests for dogs, but unwanted pregnancies can be terminated by an injection as long as this is given within 48 hours of mating.

Some females may have a false pregnancy. Sometimes they even produce milk, go into false labor and mother toys and other soft things. This situation can be left alone if only mild, but if the animal is very distressed, you should consult the vet. Sometimes a pregnant female may abort her pups. Signs of an impending abortion are bleeding from the vagina at about six weeks after mating. If this should happen, you must keep her quiet and see the vet at once.

If you want to mate a pedigreed female, there are a whole range of books on the subject to consult — the laws of genetics, studlines, and so on are far too complicated to cover here. Your vet, the breeder you bought the dog from, or the American Kennel Club may be able to tell you of a suitable mate.

The expectant mom isn't an invalid, but she should lead a quiet life without violent exercise or excitement. Take her to the vet at about 3 weeks after mating for routine prenatal checks. Feed her well with good nourishing food. Add multi-vitamins and calcium salts to her diet if the vet approves, and start preparing for the pups' arrival. Don't give her any medicine during pregnancy, although a worming dose from the vet given during pregnancy and lactation is very wise.

All this should prove a good foundation and lead up to a successful "happy event."

The happy event

Pregnancies in dogs usually average 63 days, although, as with humans, it won't matter if your dog is a few days overdue as long as she's eating well and there is no abnormal discharge. Whelping (birth) is a *very* messy business, and you won't want it to take place on your best sofa, so get the dog used to *your* chosen maternity ward well before whelping time! She needs a quiet, clean place — a box, basket or kennel will do — with lots of old newspapers as throwaway bedding.

Labor

Twenty-four hours before labor starts, her teats will usually fill out and soften with milk. Twelve hours later she'll probably start to get restless, will wander aimlessly about and prepare her bed — which will sometimes be quite different from the one you intended! She will probably also lose her appetite, pant a lot and may even vomit or have diarrhea. Sometimes this situation can go on for a day or so — with her behavior returning to normal for short intervals — but if there is no straining or abnormal discharge (i.e., bright red, greenish or smelly) you needn't worry.

This first stage of labor can last from 12-24 hours, the longer time being usual in a first pregnancy. When the second stage of labor starts, you will see forceful straining movements of the abdomen, the dog will periodically lick her genital region and some bottle-green fluid may ooze from the vulva. Start timing now — a pup should be born about an hour after this second stage starts. If no pup has appeared within two hours after straining starts, you should call the vet. Once the head and paws (possibly still enclosed in a membraneous sac) appear at the vulva, the puppy should be completely delivered within 15 minutes — if not, again call the vet. A lot of puppies are born rear legs first, but this usually causes no problems.

Delivery

Once the first puppy is born, the mother will usually break the birth sac so the pup can breathe. If she doesn't do this within a minute or two, you must, using a clean fingernail, but don't worry if the umbilical cord hasn't broken during delivery; it's not essential to break it immediately. In any case, mom usually does this while cleaning the puppy. If she hasn't got around to it after 15 minutes, tie a clean bit of cord around it and cut with sterilized scissors (see diagram).

There is usually a rest period (the third stage of labor) between each puppy — varying from 10 minutes to 2 hours. The mother may drink, clean herself and the new arrivals, perhaps even eat a little and ask to go out. All this is quite normal, and there is no standard time lapse to watch for between deliveries — instead, just remember the maximum time from the beginning of labor (straining) is two hours until the first pup appears — any longer and you should call the vet.

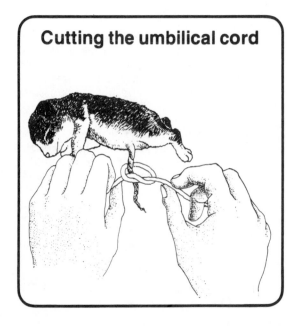

Cutting the umbilical cord

Difficult births

If a pup is showing at the vulva but is slow in popping out, you can lend mom a helping hand. Wash your hands and lubricate a finger with some petroleum jelly. Put the finger into the vagina and move it carefully around the puppy to find out where the head and legs are. If a front leg is in a backward position, you may be able to very gently pull it forward.

If the puppy seems normally placed (see picture, bottom right), get hold of it with a cloth or your bare hands, and gently pull it forward in time with each contraction. Pull on the pup's shoulders rather than his head, and pull downwards because of the angle of the vagina (see diagram).

Reviving puppies

If the mother doesn't break the birth sac a minute or so after delivery, you should by piercing it with a clean fingernail. Then hold the puppy or wrap him a towel. Support his head so it doesn't flop about, and then swing the whole pup vigorously in a wide arc from chest to knee level. His nose should point to the ground at the end of each arc to clear the airway. Then rub the puppy's face, body and chest with a rough towel. If necessary, give the kiss of life — take a breath of air, put your mouth over the puppy's nose and mouth and blow gently until the chest expands. Remove your mouth so the puppy can breathe out, and then repeat until he is breathing regularly.

When all the puppies have been delivered, offer mom a drink of milk or glucose mixed with water, and then leave the happy family to sleep in peace for a couple of hours. While they are asleep, you can prepare a clean nursing box — or at least change the bedding where they are lying. Keep the nursing box away from noise, bright light and change the bedding daily to keep it clean. You may see a brownish-red discharge from the mother's vulva, which is normal and should change to a clear mucus or disappear within a week. Any other type of discharge (bright red, greenish or greenish-black, smelly, pus-like or abnormally profuse) needs veterinary investigation. You can handle the puppies a little each day, but don't let children or strangers do so. Too much handling will make their mother nervous.

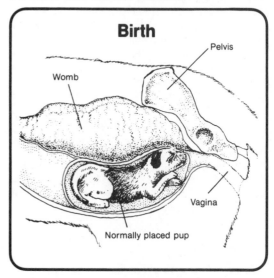

Birth

Pelvis

Womb

Vagina

Normally placed pup

Puppy rearing

Nursing females need lots of high-quality food such as meat, vegetables, and gravy, and milky foods are essential. If her milk is flowing well, the puppies should never lose weight, but if you are worried about them, weigh them every day. If the mother looks worn and thin, you may need to adjust her diet, perhaps adding a vitamin-mineral supplement, but you should check with the vet first. If she seems to be short of milk, again ask the vet — sometimes he can give her a suitable injection. If the puppies cry continuously and will not feed, call the vet before starting the demanding job of handfeeding, as this may further reduce the mother's milk flow and you'll have to take over completely.

If the pups are feeding well, remember to examine their mother's teats and clip any long hair around them — if you haven't already. Check that all the teats are being used. If any unused ones harden and swell up, massage them gently with olive oil. If she seems to have plenty of milk, but the pups aren't doing too well, the teats may not be working properly, so squeeze them gently through a bit of warm flannel until the milk flows freely. If the mother gets diarrhea but her temperature is normal and she seems otherwise well, try alternating her diet. Stop feeding dry or semi-moist foods, and instead, offer eggs and cooked white meat; e.g., chicken, tripe and fish (as long as these in themselves don't normally give her diarrhea).

Your puppies do little in life beyond eating and sleeping. If yours cry and wriggle a lot, look for signs of illness and maternal neglect (weakness, mother's inability to nurse, diarrhea, lowered body temperature) and check with the vet. Puppies are born blind and deaf. By the time they reach 10 days old their eyes will usually have opened and the ear channels follow about 2 days later. Gradually they will start to explore the world beyond their nursing box. If their eyes seem late in opening, bathe them with cotton soaked in warm water.

Your timetable for puppy rearing should be as follows:

3-4 days	Have dewclaws removed (the vet or an experienced breeder should do this). If the puppies are of a breed which has the unfortunate luck to have docked tails, this should also be done now — by the vet, of course.
3 weeks old	Offer small quantities of solid food (puppy meal or babies cereal, softened with warm milk). Don't change the pup's diet too abruptly as it may give them diarrhea.
6 weeks old	Wean the pups onto solid food, and complete this by 7 weeks at the latest. Remember, no puppy should be taken from its mother before 6 weeks. The puppies should be given five meals a day (see page 57), in amounts they can polish off in 10 minutes. Provide lots of drinking water, and worm the pups.
8 weeks old	Cut the meals down to four a day.
10 weeks old	Have all the pups vaccinated (see page 61) and re-worm. Reduce meals to three per day.
16 weeks old	Re-worm and reduce meals to two daily.
6 months	Reduce meals to one a day, or split the amount for two feeds.

As soon after the birth as possible, you should check the sex of the pups. Those you cannot find good homes for must be taken to the vet to be painlessly destroyed — **never** drown them yourself, as it is disgustingly cruel.

Rearing orphan puppies

Very occasionally a mother dog dies while she still has young pups — or is unwilling or unable to rear her puppies herself. Try, if at all possible, to find another nursing dog who can take them on — your vet may know of one. If you can't get a foster mother, you'll have to decide whether to bottle-feed the puppies yourself or ask the vet to put them to sleep. Before you opt for the former decision, take into account that bottle-feeding is a very time-consuming business and not one to be undertaken lightly.

Your orphan's nursery should be a warm, draft-free box, and if you can get hold of a baby or chicken incubator or infra-red lamp, this would be ideal. A good substitute is an electric heating pad hung down one side of the box and across a quarter of the bottom, but don't use a hot water bottle, as these are too difficult to keep at a constant and high enough temperature. Cover the pad with newspapers or thick cloths, which should be changed regularly to keep the bed clean. The temperature, which you can check by installing a wall or garden thermometer, should be 85°-88°F for the first five days of life, then about 79°F until the twentieth day. After this you can start to lower it gradually until it reads 70-74°F by the fourth week. A ticking clock hidden in their bedding will simulate their mother's heartbeat and so help them to settle down better.

As far as actually feeding them goes, you can either give them special canine milk powder (the vet will advise on this), or unsweetened evaporated milk at half the strength given to human babies, mixed with ½ teaspoonful (per pup) of medicinal glucose. **Ordinary cow's milk is no good for puppies.** Each puppy should have a teaspoonful or more of the mixture at each feed. Heat the feeding mixture to blood heat and keep it standing in a basin of hot water while feeding. You can use a fountain-pen filler or eye-dropper (a glass tube with a rubber bulb on the end), a doll's feeding bottle or a special bottle from the pet shop to give them the food. In an emergency, a twist of clean handkerchief or thin cloth dipped in the milk will be eagerly sucked by the pups — as long as it's not full of starch or detergent, of course. Don't *squeeze* the milk into the pup's mouth; let them suck it out. The pup may not cooperate very well at first but will soon get the hang of it. A good tip is to feed each pup on a covered hot-water bottle, so they can push at it with their feet while drinking.

Feed the pups every two hours during the day and every three hours at night. When the pups are 10 days old, you will pe pleased to hear that you can cut the night feeds down to one at midnight, one at 4 a.m. and one at 8 a.m., and once they reach three weeks, the pups won't need any night feeds at all. Make sure you keep all feeding utensils very clean.

To stimulate them to relieve themselves, imitate the action of their mother's tongue by massaging them with a head-to-tail motion, using a coarse towel dipped in warm water and well wrung out. Especially remember to use a circular action on their belly. To clean the pups, dab them with cotton dipped in mild antiseptic, then dry them thoroughly and dust their abdomens and rears with baby talc. Eventually, they should start to wash themselves.

You'll have to keep their bedding clean until they are about three weeks old. Then when they begin to stagger about, start to wean them.

Points to consider

If you're thinking about getting a dog, don't just march out and buy the first one you see or, worse, be bowled over by that cute little puppy in the pet shop. A dog should be a considered purchase so both of you will live happily together. Here are some points you should think about before taking the plunge:

- **Is there somebody at home most of the day?** If the whole family is out at work or school, it's really not fair to a dog who will need lots of company and exercise. You'd do better to keep a cat, a more natural 'loner', though even he needs *some* company.
- **How much room have you?** It's pretty silly to try to keep a Great Dane in a small apartment — and disposing of feces can be a problem, too!
- **Where will you exercise the dog?** If you don't have a suitably large garden or open space nearby where he can run free, you'd do better with a small breed that needs less exercise. A small dog, too, is much cheaper to feed.
- **Can you afford one?** When deciding to buy remember, apart from spending quite a bit each week on food, even the healthiest dog will run up veterinary bills from time to time. Necessary vaccinations, the cost of kennels should you go away on vacation, odd problems — let alone a serious illness, which, of course, you hope won't happen but may — all cost money. *So can you afford his keep?*
- **What sex, too?** A female will come into heat after about 6 months and have regular seasons for the rest of her life — during which time she will be courted by a posse of canine admirers who'll drool over your doorstep.
- **Never get a dog — or indeed any pet — as just another "toy" for your children to play with.** Children have to understand the responsibility of looking after a pet's needs properly, and it's good for them to start learning this at an early age. However, for much of the dog's life **you** will have to be responsible for its welfare — it's no use kidding yourself otherwise.
- **Different municipalities have different legislation about the liabilites and duties of dog-keepers.** Make sure you know whether you are legally responsible or not for your dog's action, whether it needs a license or must wear a collar, whether you have to report running over a dog, and so on.

Needless to say, there are also laws about cruelty to dogs, as with other animals. Some countries like Australia and Britain have severe quarantine laws to protect their own animals against disease, whereby imported dogs and other appropriate animals must be kept in quarantine for a suitable period. So if you're planning to move abroad or have to travel overseas a lot, find out how you stand with regard to these laws. It's not worth buying a dog if you have to leave it behind 6 months out of 12 or worse, in quarantine.

Think of these points over carefully, and if you then decide to buy a dog, you must consider where you're going to buy him. Well, obviously you can go to a breeder for a pedigreed dog. Some breeders advertise in newspapers, or you may know someone who has puppies and is anxious to find them good homes. For a mongrel — or even an abandoned pedigreed dog — your nearest pound or animal welfare organization is bound to have scores of dogs which are facing a painless, but nevertheless unnecessary death unless good homes are found for them. Usually, such animals have had a veterinary check for soundness, and it is customary to make a small donation to the charity. Some pet shops sell puppies, but make sure the shop is clean, smells fresh, and that the pups look healthy and happy. Never buy from a back street shop or a market — and never buy a puppy younger than 10 weeks old. By that age it should be fully weaned and on a mixed diet.

Look any dog over for general health (see page 10), get the vet to check him over as soon as you can and at the proper time take him to be vaccinated. Get your dog a basket, collar, leash, name disc and something to chew on (other than your slippers), and you are set for 15 years or so of happy, healthy companionship and loyalty.

Dogs and other animals

Dogs *can live* in reasonable tolerance, if not always friendship, with other pets, provided you introduce them carefully. As far as possible, introduce the stronger animal to the weaker, and make sure the weaker is on its own ground. If you are introducing a puppy into a household which already has a cat, cut the cat's claws first. The cat will probably initially resent the pup, but after a while, they should settle down and tolerate each other if you prevent injuries in the meantime. Use individual feeding dishes, and as with all animals, try to prevent them from having a confrontation, which will cause them to harbor permanent hostilities towards each other. Try also to be fair and equal with your attention so neither animal becomes jealous. If at all possible, introduce two traditionally mutual enemies — e.g., cat and dog — into your household at the same time, so neither has a territorial advantage. A small pet, such as a guinea pig, should not be touched by the dog if you make it very clear the small animal is yours and not to be interfered with. This can apply to even smaller creatures, like hamsters and birds, but you had better keep them under your supervision and not leave them alone with the dog.

Household hazards

Although you may not realize it, your house is probably full of things which can constitute a danger to your dog. Insecticides, rat poisons and weedkillers are obvious dangers and all should be kept out of his way. Electric wires are very likely to be chewed by puppies, so keep them well out of reach.

Quite ordinary objects, such as string, toys, rubber bands, etc., may be dangerous if gobbled up by the investigative dog! None of these hazards, however, need deter you from keeping a dog. Patient training and a watchful eye should ensure that your chosen animal is well able to steer clear of trouble.

Moving with a dog

Make sure the dog is carefully shut up well before the movers arrive. Either put him on a leash or, in a pinch, in a room not to be cleared until last — with a large label indicating his presence on the door. At the new home, don't let him out of doors unless the yard is secure, and exercise him on a leash if in doubt.

Which breed for you?

You've considered all the points outlined on the previous pages — and you still *really* want a dog! So now you have to decide which breed to have. Well, apart from considerations such as size and character, the choice really depends on you. What do you want the dog to be — just a pet, a companion, a guard dog or good breeding stock? Remember, too, that pedigreed dogs may look great, but they can often have inbuilt genetic health problems — blindness in poodles is a case in point. They'll cost a lot to buy, too — even one which will never star at a national dog show. All in all, unless you really fall in love with a particular breed or want to breed show dogs, you'd do just as well with a lovable mongrel. They are cheaper, easy to come by at a dog pound, just as affectionate — and often much, much healthier. If you decide that a pedigree is the dog for you, then you'll have to decide which breed. Needless to say, there are hundreds to choose from, but again, the final choice rests with you.

The following may help you narrow the list down, as it splits the main and most popular breeds up into their different types; i.e., working dogs as opposed to toy breeds.

Non-Sporting Dogs
Alaskan Malamute
Bernese Mountain Dog
Boston Terrier
Boxer
British Bulldog
Bull Mastiff
Chow Chow
Dalmatian
Doberman Pinscher
French Bulldog
Giant Schnauzer
Great Dane
Keeshund
Lhaso Apso
Mastiff
Poodle
Pyrenean Mountain Dog
Rottweiler
Samoyed
Schipperke
Schnauzer
Shih Tzu
Siberian Husky
St. Bernard
Tibetan Spaniel
Tibetan Terrier

Toy Dogs
Affenpinscher
Australian Silky Terrier
Bichon Frise
Cavalier King Charles Spaniel
Chihuahua
Chinese Crested Dog
English Toy Terrier (Black & Tan)
Griffon Bruxellois
Italian Greyhound
Japanese Chin
King Charles Spaniel
Lowchen
Maltese
Miniature Pinscher
Miniature Poodle
Papillon
Pekinese
Pomeranian
Pug
Yorkshire Terrier

Dalmatian

Labrador

Dachshund

Sporting Terriers
Airedale Terrier
Australian Terrier
Bedlington Terrier
Border Terrier
Bull Terrier
Cairn Terrier
Dandie Dinmont Terrier
Fox Terrier
Irish Terrier
Kerry Blue Terrier

Lakeland Terrier
Manchester Terrier
Norfolk Terrier
Norwich Terrier
Scottish Terrier
Sealyham Terrier
Skye Terrier
Staffordshire Bull Terrier
Welsh Terrier
West Highland White Terrier

Hunting dogs
Brittany Spaniel
Clumber Spaniel
Cocker Spaniel
Curly Coated Retriever
English Setter
English Springer Spaniel
Flat Coated Retriever
German Short-haired Pointer
German Wire-hired Pointer
Golden Retriever
Gordon Setter
Hungarian Viszla
Irish Setter
Irish Water Spaniel
Labrador
Pointer
Weimaraner
Welsh Springer Spaniel
Field Spaniel

Hound Dogs
Afghan Hound
Basenji
Basset Griffon Vendeen
Basset Hound
Beagle
Bloodhound
Borzoi
Dachshund
Deerhound
Elkhound
Finnish Spitz
Foxhound
Greyhound
Harrier
Irish Wolfhound
Japanese Spitz
Pharoah Hound
Rhodesian Ridgeback
Saluki
Whippet

Airedale terrier

Collie

Working Dogs
Australian Cattle Dog
Australian Kelpie
Bearded Collie
Belgian Shepherd Dog
Border Collie
Bouvier des Flandres
Briard
Collie
German Shepherd Dog (Alsatian)
Hungarian Puli
Norwegian Buhund
Old English Sheepdog
Welsh Corgi

Yorkshire terrier

A dog's life?

It's not difficult to maintain your dog in good condition throughout his life, provided you take a little trouble. Good food, clean water, regular exercise and inoculations, an eye kept on his health, plus your companionship, should all help your lively pup to reach a ripe and contented old age.

Sleeping quarters

Give your puppy a draft-free bed or basket, raised slightly above the ground, with layers of newspaper as bedding. This should be changed frequently so the bed is kept clean and, also, to prevent it from becoming a flea haven. A newly-acquired pup will sometimes settle down more happily beside a hotwater bottle wrapped well in a thick towel — and his first few nights will be less traumatic if you give him a ticking clock to remind him of his mom's heartbeat. Put him in his bed and shut the door on him, then harden

your heart against his howls. If you give in and go back, he'll expect attention every time thereafter. Once puppyhood is over, you should make sure his bed is big enough for him or, of course, you could give him a kennel out of doors.

For a kennel, the size should be as follows: minimum length — the length of the dog plus half its breadth; minimum breadth — twice the dog's breadth; minimum height — the standing height of the dog, to the top of his head. Make sure the kennel has well-insulated walls and roof, with the floor raised a little way off the ground. Naturally, it should be draft-proof, dry and easy to clean. The door should be just big enough for the dog. Give him some disposable bedding; i.e., straw. Remember, if your dog does have a kennel out-of-doors there may still be times when he will need to be kept inside — if he becomes very ill for instance — so it's a good idea to have a bed that he can use.

Toilet training

As soon as the puppy starts to eat any solid food, you should start house-training him. This takes great patience, but your puppy will usually be eager to please you. If you praise him when he gets it right, he'll soon get the message. Never punish him for slowness or an accident, and certainly don't "rub his nose in it," but just give him a firm "No" when he makes a mess. Rubbing his nose in it won't teach him anything, just confuse him.

About 15 minutes after his meals, and first thing in the morning and last thing at night, put him in a suitable lavatory spot in the yard. It's a good idea to have plenty of newspaper around while he's learning, and if he does have an accident indoors, clean it up immediately and spray the area with an aerosol deodorant to prevent his being attracted back to the same spot and tempted to repeat the action.

and milk products are good, too, but if your dog gets diarrhea and perhaps vomits, take milk off his menu and see if that is the cause. Cereals or dog biscuits are good, and vegetables are invaluable, providing you get the dog used to them early on. Dogs don't actually need fruit, as their bodies manufacture vitamin C naturally, but it can be useful.

Lovely grub!

When you get a new pup, he will probably be about 8-10 weeks old and need 4 meals a day.

A good diet would be:

Breakfast	Bowl of cereal, baby or puppy meal with milk
Midday Meal	Chopped canned dog food or semi-moist food
Snack	Milk, plus a repeat of midday meal
Evening Meal	Same as midday plus cereal with milk

Give him a vitamin pill or drops each day and, of course, lots of fresh drinking water. Vary the brands of store-bought food so he doesn't get hooked on any one kind. And reduce the meals to three a day at 12 weeks and two at 16 weeks. Dogs *can* make do with one main meal a day, but two are probably better (equal parts both night and morning). Feed the dog regularly with freshly prepared food in clean dishes.

For the adult dog, canned food is very convenient, but you may occasionally give him fresh food as a change. Meat may be given cooked or raw, but make sure any raw meat given is bought fresh from the butcher to minimize the risk of infection. Organ meat, such as liver or kidney, should never be fed raw. Meat should contain both fat and lean — and although liver is good for protein, it shouldn't exceed 5% of your dog's weekly diet, as it can be too strong for some stomachs. Cooked fish is excellent, but remove the bones from larger fish. Cheese

Bones

Most dogs adore bones, but feeding them is of doubtful value. They don't actually clean the teeth and can occasionally cause digestive problems. If you decide to feed bones, make sure they are big bones, not splintery ones from chicken or rabbit, etc., although you may find that even big marrow bones will have an adverse effect on some dogs; i.e., constipation or even a blockage of the intestine.

How much to feed?

Dogs vary so much in size that it is difficult to state the exact amount of food they should have, but a good rule of thumb is that the daily amount of meat should be about ½ oz. a day per pound of body weight for a young dog, and ⅓ oz. for fully-grown dogs. With canned food, give ½-¾ can per day for toy breeds, ¾-1½ cans for small breeds, 1½-2½ cans for medium-size dogs and 2½-4 cans for large breeds. (The cans mentioned are the large-size ones.) With dry foods (a balanced meal), give an average of 4¼ oz. for a 5-lb. dog, 9½ oz. for 25-lb. dog and a little more than 1 lb. for a 70-lb. dog. Semi-moist complete food should be fed as ½-¾ packets for a 5-lb. dog, 1½-2½ packets for a 25-lb. dog and 2½-4 packets for a 70-lb. dog.

All the above amounts depend not only on the dog's size, but also on his daily activity; i.e., a working dog as opposed to a household pet — and also on his tendency to obesity. Make sure that your dog doesn't become overweight.

A dog's life?

Walks

One of the joys of owning a dog is taking it for walks — although the pleasure may sometimes fall on a dreadful wet night! All dogs need some exercise, and big dogs need a great deal, as do some very active terriers. Walks must be regular (twice daily) and ideally in different places to keep the dog's interest. Never take your dog out if he's not wearing a collar, partly because of the legal requirements and also because it's a useful thing to grab him by should you ever need to. You'll also legally need to put him on a leash for walks in many areas, and a harness can be useful for some dogs.

If you're training your dog, a choke chain and leash may be used. In this case, make sure the chain leading from the loop is at the back of the dog's neck, or it may damage his throat and restrict breathing.

Training

A well trained dog usually means a happy dog — and certainly a happy owner. If you are patient and consistent, and start early on, most dogs learn easily. Remember you are their pack leader, and they are anxious for your approval. Start training when your puppy is about three months old, and always discourage such anti-social activities as chasing cars, bicycles or, worse still, farm animals! Use tidbits as rewards for good behavior, and scold very thoroughly when the dog misbehaves. Certainly never hit him; the cross tone of your voice should be sufficient and he will then link your command with a punishment. Never punish a dog in any other way. Don't try to teach the dog too much at a time, and *short* daily lessons are best. Use a firm tone of voice and the same word every time for each command you give.

Follow the points below and the diagram on the left for your own dog-training program.

1 Sit   Before a meal, take the dog on his leash into a quiet room. Say "Sit" in a firm voice and push down on his rear end. Reward and praise.

2 Down   When he will sit of his own accord, get him to do so then press his shoulder and say "Down" while pulling his forelegs forward. Reward and praise.

3 Stay   Put the dog on a long leash and make him sit. Move away from him saying "Stay." Continue practicing this until the dog will stay where he is without the leash. Reward and praise each time he stays.

4 Come   Call the dog by name. Reward and praise when he comes. If the dog is running about and refuses to come, don't scold him when you eventually succeed in making him obey. If you do, he will associate the "coming" with punishment. Praise him instead.

5 Heel   Hold the leash slack in your right hand and walk with the dog on your left side. Say "Heel" as you move forward, patting the dog when he responds.

6 Fetch   Many dogs, especially of a retrieving breed, will do this naturally, but a dog that you have to train to do this should first be fully trained in staying, sitting and coming to you.

Bathing

Although grooming a dog once or twice a week is essential to keep his coat free from dirt and loose hairs, and also as a check against parasites, baths are necessary only when the dog has become incredibly dirty. Most dogs are less than enthusiastic about being bathed, and you may need a helper to hold the dog on a leash while you administer the bath! Wearing a plastic coat backwards is a good way of keeping yourself reasonably dry. Use some receptacle large enough — a bath, sink or basin depending on the size of the dog — and before you begin, add a few drops of vegetable oil to the dog's eyes to prevent irritation. Then wet the dog all over with *lukewarm* water, keeping his eyes, ears and muzzle dry, before applying a mild shampoo, never detergent. Rinse carefully with warm water from a big jug until all the shampoo has gone. Dry him with a towel and keep him in a warm room until he is absolutely bone dry.

Balls and other toys

Many dogs adore running after and catching balls, sticks and so on and will continue to want to run after them long after you have tired of throwing them! A retrieving type of dog will positively *need* to bring the object back to you! At home, a chewing toy which is the dog's alone can be useful to prevent your slippers from becoming the object of his attentions, especially if he's a young dog.

A dog's life?

Collars

In towns and cities it is illegal to let a dog out without a collar and disc displaying the owner's name and address. In any case, a collar is invaluable, as you can not only add a disc with your address and telephone number, but can use the collar to grab an injured, frightened or just straying dog. Get the dog used to collar and leash while he is still a puppy — see page 58. You may also like to fit him out with a flea collar, although not everyone believes that they actually work!

Travel sickness

Many dogs suffer from travel sickness, but you can do your best to prevent it by following the points outlined below.

1. Get the dog (ideally when he's still a puppy) accustomed to sitting in a stationary car.
2. Then take him on very short trips, gradually increasing their length until he's used to traveling in this way.
3. Don't feed him before a journey.
4. Human travel sickness tablets can be helpful, but check dosage with your vet first.

Remember it's best not to let the dog ride with his head out of the car window, as often this sets up eye irritations and other ailments, apart from the danger that he may be hit or jump out!

Grooming

Unlike cats, dog's don't really groom themselves, so you should groom your dog regularly to keep his skin and coat healthy. Look at his skin every week and remove any loose hairs. Clean his ears, too, especially if he's a long-eared breed. Most dogs are healthy creatures, but you should give them the "once-over" regularly and get to know their appearance and habits so you can quickly spot anything unusual.

Here is a dog-management routine that takes care of most points:

Daily	Groom dog. Observe his general appearance, attitude to life, appetite and activity. Any change, and you should investigate further.
Weekly	Check through fur and skin for external parasites (see page 18). Examine and clean ears (page 14).
Monthly	Clean teeth if necessary (page 24).
Every two weeks	Check claw length and appearance, and trim if necessary (page 22).
Annually	Booster shots and check-up at vet's.

Old Age

Like elderly human beings, dogs gradually start wearing out, although they may live a long time (over 17 — and they're doing quite well). Rather than the traditional "1 year in a dog's life equals 7 years in man's," it's more realistic to use the sliding scale of comparison worked out by a French veterinarian, Dr. Lebeau. With this, the first year of the dog's life equals 15 human years, his second year equals 9 and thereafter each dog year equals 4 human years. So a 15 year old dog is 76 in human terms and a 17 year old is 84!

To ensure your dog at least reaches his 70 years, you should, above all, keep his weight down. A "slimline" dog is usually a healthy dog — obesity leads to heart trouble, joint disease, liver problems and diabetes. So make sure your dog is sleek enough to show *definitely separated* chest and abdominal areas. When his waistline starts to spread, cut down on starch and carbohydrates and withdraw milk from his diet.

The easiest way to weigh your dog is for you to pick him up and then stand on the bathroom scale. Then weigh yourself and deduct your own weight. Elderly dogs often get a bit thin, eat a lot more (or a lot less) and become more thirsty as their livers and kidneys wear out. If you suspect kidney trouble (see page 32) check with the vet, who can often prescribe a suitable diet and drugs to help the senior citizen carry on reasonably well. Old dogs may also get constipated, so add lots of bulky fiber to their diet and an occasional "opening" dose of liquid paraffin. They may smell a bit, too, but the vet can often help with this. The mouth is the most common place to start smelling, but other causes are ears (especially in long-eared breeds like spaniels) and rear ends! Make sure the dog's rear hair is clipped short so it doesn't get soiled. A general, all-over, non-specific odor may be "old dog smell" from his coat — so bathe him every two weeks with an ordinary human shampoo with selenium in it. Now that his courting and territorial days are over, he may get less fussy about his appearance, and you may have to supplement his grooming.

Watch over your aging dog's teeth carefully, and catch tartar before it has a chance to build up. However, if grandpa dog does lose all his teeth, he can still make out all right if you cut his food up for him. Eyesight and hearing may also start to fail and the elderly dog may occasionally be incontinent. He may also get a bit cantankerous and grumble at having to go for a walk on a rainy night. Remember to fuss over him a bit more, just as you would a respected old gentleman, keep up all his vaccination boosters and watch over his health with care.

Finally, if your vet says he is rather too old or feeble to be contented or pain-free, you should brace yourself to give him the last favor of a dignified and painless end. If you can, stay with the dog to reassure him while the vet gives him a painless injection — and soon his troubles will be over.

Vaccination

You absolutely must protect your dog or puppy regularly with the right inoculations against the killers distemper, contagious canine hepatitis, rabies, two forms of leptospirosis and canine parvovirus — see page 45. Vaccination time begins when the dog is 10 weeks old unless the vet advises it earlier because of some local infection. The rabies vaccine is usually given at the age of four months. Some vaccinations may have to be repeated at 12 weeks and must be boosted annually thereafter. Your vet will give you a schedule. Until a pup's vaccination is complete, keep him well away from other dogs, as well as the streets and parks. Try not to let people outside the family handle him either.

You should get a certificate confirming your dog's vaccination. Keep it safe — it's not only a good reminder for when the next shots are due, but you'll have to produce an up-to-date certificate before the dog is admitted to a boarding kennel.

Fascinating facts

- Dogs (and wolves and foxes) are descended from a small, weasel-like mammal called *Miacis,* which was a tree-dwelling creature and existed about 40 million years ago. Dogs, as we know them today, first appeared in Eurasia about 13,000 years ago and were probably a direct descendant of a small, grey wolf (not from the type of jackal or jackal/wolf as previously thought). Dogs were first domesticated by cavemen in the Paleolithic age and gradually developed (or were bred) into the breeds known today.

- The tallest dogs are the Great Dane and the Irish wolfhound. The largest Great Dane stood at 40.5 in. and an Irish wolfhound 39.5 in.

- The heaviest dog was a St. Bernard weighing 305 lbs. The smallest dogs are the Chihuahua, the Yorkshire terrier and the toy poodle. A Yorkie once weighed in at only 10 oz.

- Dogs have been used as guards, hunters, eyes for the blind, drug and explosives detectors, rodent controllers — and even weapons! In Roman times and the Middle Ages, mastiffs wearing light armor, carrying spikes and pots of flaming sulfur and resin, ran into battle against mounted knights. In World War II the Russians trained dogs to run suicide missions between the tracks of German tanks with mines strapped on their backs.

- Dogs' hearing is very acute. They can register sounds of 35,000 vibrations a second (compared to our 20,000 and a cat's 25,000).

- Dogs naturally have a wonderful sense of smell. They have many more sensory "smelling" cells than a man's 5,000,000. A dachshund has 125,000,000, a fox terrier 147,000,000 and an Alsation (often used as a "sniffer" dog) has 220,000,000. Truffle hounds can find the fungus delicacy even when it's a foot underground.

- The oldest reliable age recorded for a dog is 29 years, 5 months for a Queensland "heeler" called Bluey in Victoria, Australia. The average dog lives to around 15 years of age.

Arthritis
Inflammation of the joints — usually affecting one joint, occasionally more.

Bronchitis
Inflammation of the bronchial tubes; usually accompanied by other infections of the respiratory system.

Canker
General term applied to infection/inflammation of the ear. Usually involves a discharge.

Cataract
Degeneration of eye lens, causing it to become opaque.

Conjunctivitis
Inflammation of membrane lining the eye.

Cystitis
Inflammation of the bladder.

Diabetes
Sugar diabetes occurs when the pancreas fails to produce sufficient insulin to assist the body in absorbing sugar. Water diabetes occurs due to a rare malfunction of the pituitary gland within the brain and results in excessive urination due to loss of control over the kidneys.

Eczema
General term applied to a skin condition, usually sudden in onset and often self-inflicted.

Gastritis
Inflammation of the stomach.

Gingivitis
Inflammation of the gums.

Glaucoma
Painful increase of pressure inside eye — often resulting in blindness.

Hematoma
Blood blister resulting from accumulation of blood due to burst blood vessel. Often caused through excessive scratching or from a blow to the body.

Hip dysplasia
A condition found in large breeds of dog, though most usually associated with German Shepherd dogs. Lameness and instability of the hind legs result from poorly formed ball and socket joint at hip.

Intussusception
A serious condition affecting young puppies whereby a section of the intestine telescopes, into a wider section.

Laryngitis
Inflammation of the larynx.

Mange
Disease of the fur and skin resulting from a variety of different mange mites — all of which produce different symptoms and affect particular areas of the body; i.e. head, ears, etc.

Mastitis
Inflammation of the mammary glands (teats).

Metritis
Inflammation of the uterus — usually due to infection of the uterus from outside.

Middle ear disease
Inflammation of the middle ear behind ear drum — otherwise known as Otitis Media.

Nephritis
Inflammation of the kidneys.

Pyometritis
Purulent inflammation of the uterus.

Rhinitis
Inflammation of the lining of the nose.

Rickets
Severe bone deformity in young dogs caused by dietary imbalance.

Sinusitis
Inflammation of the sinus cavities.

Tonsillitis
Inflammation of the tonsils.

Vaginitis
Inflammation of the vagina — usually caused by an infection entering from the dog's outside environment.

Index